DEMOCRACY
And
ARAB POLITICAL CULTURE

Elie Kedourie

FRANK CASS

Published in 1994 in Great Britain by
FRANK CASS & CO. LTD.
Gainsborough House, Gainsborough Road,
London E11 1RS, England

and in the United States of America by
FRANK CASS
c/o International Specialized Book Services, Inc.
5804 N.E. Hassalo Street, Portland, Oregon 97213-3644

Copyright © 1994 The Estate of Elie Kedourie
(second edition with corrections)

British Library Cataloguing in Publication Data

Kedourie, Elie
  Democracy and Arab Political Culture. –
  2Rev.ed
  I. Title
  321.809174927

  ISBN 0-7146-4509-5

Library of Congress Cataloging in Publication Data

Kedourie. Elie.
  Democracy and Arab political culture / Elie Kedourie. — 2nd ed.
with corrections.
    p.   cm.
  ISBN 0-7146-4509-5
  1. Democracy–Arab countries. 2. Political culture–Arab
countries. 3. Arab countries–Politics and government—1945-
I. Title
JQ1850.A91K43   1994
  321.8'09174927—dc20   93-4779
                                                                CIP

Democracy and Arab Political Culture was originally published by the
Washington Institute for Near East Policy.

Printed in Great Britain by
Redwood Books, Trowbridge, Wiltshire

Contents

Preface to the Second Edition

 Elie Kedourie wrote this monograph while in residence at the Washington Institute for Near East Policy. His residence there was of four months just before the outbreak of the Gulf War in January 1991, and two months in the summer of 1991, when talk of democracy was on everyone's lips. People seemed to believe that the introduction of democracy would cure many of the problems in the Middle East, and were surprised and shocked when the Algerian elections showed that constitutional representation could bring forward 'the baddies', in this case the fundamentalists, the *bêtes noires par excellence*. Elie tried to show that, contrary to general belief, democracy and constitutional government had been tried but failed. It failed for the reasons that he brings out in this monograph.

The book is deceptively simple. It does, however, encapsulate a lifetime of study and thought. Elie has written extensively about the history of the Middle East from the time when he published his first book, *England and the Middle East: The Destruction of the Ottoman Empire* in 1956. This book marked a milestone in the interpretation and the study of the history of the region. It was a seminal work, one of many, which gradually influenced and fashioned public opinion in spite of a whole cabal which was always ready to attack him.

It is relevant to quote what he himself wrote about *England and the Middle East*:

> My work at St. Antony's resulted in a book which I finished writing in December 1953 and which was published in April 1956 . . . . It was an enterprise of some temerity since it was by no means evident when the plan of the book took shape in my mind that I would have enough evidence at my disposal to enable me to produce a consecutive and

coherent account which, if it could not be comprehensive
– and it could not then possibly be – would at least show
the reader where the gaps and the obscurities lay. Two
things may be pleaded in palliation of my temerity. In the
first place, accounts of Middle East history in the first world
war then extant were unsatisfactory. They were generally
incurious and uncritical, and (what was worse) either plain
(or disguised) political advocacy, or else unwittingly tain-
ted with political *parti pris*. In the second place, though the
evidence was not as abundant as it became when the British
archives were opened after 1966, a close examination dis-
closed quite a respectable body of materials available for
the historian's scrutiny.

Elie goes on to explain how he worked from published
material, scrutinising and comparing memoirs, eye-witness
accounts, official publications, Arabic chronicles and memoirs,
and so on, and how this led to a study other than one of
received judgement. He used this method throughout his
working life. However, he did not confine himself to writing
about the Middle East. His *Nationalism*, first published in
1960, and now reprinted by Blackwell's in a new expanded
edition, was as influential then as it is relevant today. Other
books, too many to enumerate here, followed. His numerous
articles and book reviews are scattered in many newspapers
and academic journals. In October 1964, he found an enter-
prising and courageous publisher, Frank Cass, who undertook
to publish another project next to his heart, *Middle Eastern
Studies*, a journal now in its thirtieth year and being edited on
the same principles.

This began a happy and fruitful working relationship.
Middle Eastern Studies was the first of many scholarly journals
to be published by Frank Cass, and it was Elie Kedourie's
influence that set the high academic standards for all the
journals that followed.

From his first appointment at the London School of
Economics and Political Science in 1953 to his retirement in
1990, he taught the history of political thought. Although he
supervised many theses in Middle Eastern history and called

himself a historian, his interest in political philosophy and his devotion to and care for his students never took second place. His forthcoming book on Hegel and Marx will show an aspect of this dimension of his learning.

During several periods abroad, he taught in many places but mainly at Princeton, Harvard and Brandeis Universities. He greatly enjoyed being a visiting fellow at The Netherlands Institute for Advanced Studies (1980–81) and at All Souls College, Oxford (1989–90), as well as in several other places where he spent shorter periods.

His influence was felt not only in the field of history. As one commentator put it: 'He was also one of the most influential thinkers in the revival of conservative political thought which prepared the way for the electoral successes of the British Conservative Party.' But Elie was never a member of any political party. His two pamphlets *Diamonds into Glass* (1988) and *Perestroika in the Universities* (1989) are a powerful attack on the educational policies of Mrs Thatcher's government.

During the last year of his life which he spent so happily at the Woodrow Wilson Center for International Scholars in Washington, he was engaged on what was to be his *magnum opus*, a study of Conservatism. This, alas, will not see the light of day.

Both his election to The British Academy in 1975 and his CBE in 1991 came as most pleasurable surprises. His modesty and reserve did not predispose him to seek or to expect such honours. He received his honorary doctorate from Tel Aviv University in 1991 in the same spirit.

May he long rest in peace.

Sylvia Kedourie
London, December 1993

Preface

 The collapse of the Soviet bloc and the end of the Cold War have come almost too swiftly to be registered. As Czechoslovakia's dissident-turned-President Vaclav Havel has said, one no longer has even the time to be astonished. No less striking than the demise of Soviet power has been the global sweep of the democratic idea as more and more societies, from Uruguay to the Ukraine to Tiananmen Square, after the long hiatus of dictatorship, take the first steps toward realizing the Enlightenment ideals of democratic self-government first enunciated in the American Revolution.

Yet as striking as this global democratic revolution has been, equally striking has been its failure thus far to stir the Middle East. Indeed, except for democratic Israel, the Middle East seems to be the only region in the world untouched by the democratic revolution sweeping the globe. Throughout the Middle East, despotisms of various hues hold sway. Where limited forms of democracy have been introduced, in Jordan and Algeria, the result has been electoral support for fundamentalist forces, whose commitment to democracy is either questionable or non-existent.

This phenomenon cries out for explanation, and few are better equipped to offer that than the author of this monograph, Professor Elie Kedourie, one of the master scholars of modern Middle Eastern history. Through his long and prolific career Professor Kedourie has skillfully combined deep knowledge, sober analysis and elegant prose to produce a shelf of volumes that will long endure as classics of Middle Eastern studies. His hallmark learning, perspicacity and grace are abundantly in evidence in this study of democracy and Arab political culture.

True to his calling, Professor Kedourie approaches this subject historically, examining the political traditions of Islam, the introduction of Western ideas in the 19th century and the ways in which those ideas took root, or failed to do so, in the region. He deftly places the vicissitudes of the present in the context of the enduring influence of the past.

As we look toward a new, post-Cold War world, Professor Kedourie's masterful *tour d'horizon* will prove valuable to policy makers, scholars and laymen who wish to better understand the tangled ideas and tragic conflicts that have bedeviled the Middle East and undermined progress down to our own time.

Barbi Weinberg
President
February 1992

Introduction: Democracy and the Middle Eastern Political Tradition

 In May 1991, the Cairo newspaper *al-Ahram* conducted an opinion poll which was said to cover a cross-section of the Arab world. The poll was designed to discover what kind of political arrangements Arabs preferred to see in their countries. We, of course, do not know to what extent the 4,997 who were polled are an accurate mirror of public opinion. At any rate, the results, for what they are worth, showed that 56% favored the introduction of Western-style democracy, while 52.3% demanded the application of the *Sharia* which would involve a ban on alcohol and gambling, and the introduction of Islamic punishments!

While the preference for rule according to the *Sharia* and what it would involve is intelligible both to outside observers and to the respondents themselves, it is by no means clear what the parallel preference for democracy can mean to them, or how we ourselves may understand the significance of this preference. Nor is it easy for us to understand how so many of the respondents could reconcile preference for democracy with preference for a *Sharia*-governed polity.

To hold simultaneously ideas which are not easily reconcilable argues, then, a deep confusion in the Arab public mind, at least about the meaning of democracy. The confusion is, however, understandable since the idea of democracy is quite alien to the mind-set of Islam. Democracy is, in any case, today, itself by no means a clear or precise notion.

Classical Muslim philosophers would have had no difficulty in supplying a meaning for the word democracy— a meaning with which they would have become familiar from their study of the Greek philosophers, and particularly Aristotle. For it is the Greek political experience, the experience of the *polis*, which was theorized by these Greek thinkers. Plato and Aristotle notably assigned a place for this concept in their political typology and described the characteristics of this kind of rule. Democracy, for them, was a low and degraded regime in which the masses, moved by their passions and appetites, sought to exercise unrestrained power. For the Greek thinkers, as for their Muslim disciples, democracy signified despotism—a hydra-headed despotism, certainly no better, and perhaps worse, than the despotism of one man. In the scheme sketched out in Plato's *Republic*, the rule of the philosopher-king degenerates into a timocracy, then into an oligarchy and finally into a democracy—a regime which sets the scene and prepares the way for the advent of a tyrant who puts a stop to democratic lawlessness and arbitrariness.

That democracy was an undesirable and abhorrent regime remained a commonplace both in the Muslim world and in the Christian West, and this continued to be the case until the downfall of the old regime in Europe and the great wave of populist and radical political ideas which accompanied revolutions on both sides of the Atlantic.

"Democracy" began then to lose somewhat its pejorative connotations and to be used increasingly to describe a polity in which sovereignty was unambiguously located in the citizen body. It is such a state of affairs which people have in mind when they praise democracy and recommend it to those parts of the world which are now deprived of its blessings. Nevertheless, as has been said, democracy remains an ambiguous and imprecise word with which to describe political arrangements which now generally obtain in the Western world, and which are recommended to, say, Africa or the Middle East. Until very recently there was a class of states which called themselves peoples' democracies. Apart from the pleonasm of which the expression is guilty, it is also the case that the democratic regime here in question is worlds away from what is understood when the United States is called a democracy. It is this kind of ambiguity attached to the term which makes one wonder what the respondents to the poll conducted by *al-Ahram* could have understood by the democracy for which they expressed so decisive a preference.

Democracy, when used to describe a polity like the United States, has implicit in it a whole complex of ideas which must be made explicit if we are fully to appreciate the gulf which separates modern and ancient democracies, and if we are to judge whether the concepts and practices of modern democracies can be acclimatized and can take root in countries where other political traditions have predominated.

The modern idea of democracy is inseparable from the idea of the state. The idea of the state began to acquire its present meaning during the early modern period of European history. It connotes a particular piece of territory which is under sovereign power. Sovereignty has come to be understood as an impersonal public rule from which is derived the title of a government to govern, regardless of its character. Sovereignty, then, is the source of all political authority. As it was gradually worked out in Europe, through various disputes and conflicts, the impersonal idea of sovereignty came to be seen to rule out two ideas hitherto widely prevalent. First, that force or conquest gives title to rule, and second, that rulers are by God appointed. It came to be realized that to ground rule on force makes neither for stability nor for legitimacy, while divine appointment can be indifferently claimed by those in power as by those who may succeed in supplanting them, since the only sign of divine approval is that the ruler does have—so long as he has it—the power to rule. Sovereignty, then, comes to be distinguished from mere force, as from divine prescription. It is seen as the impersonal and invariable foundation of public authority which gives legitimacy to a government.

How, then, does it arise? The inescapable answer is that it arises from popular consent.

The ideas which are thus associated with the modern notion of the state remain, however, mere abstractions unless they are embodied in manners of behavior, in procedures, laws and institutions. The consent from which sovereignty derives has to have a way, in other words, of expressing itself in order to confer legitimacy on the government in a manner which is both public and rule-governed. In large and complex modern societies this consent can be conferred only through parliamentary institutions which **represent** the people and give public assent in recognized, proper and regular forms to laws and to the acts of government. The idea of popular sovereignty would otherwise have remained quite empty of content. That it has not done so in the Western world is due to the device of representation—a device invented for other purposes in the medieval West, and which is one of a handful of original devices in the history of government to have been invented and perfected.

Representation implies elections and elections imply voting. In the modern West, it has become accepted and established that every citizen shall have one, and no more than one, vote. "One man, one vote," however, by no means implies that the citizens are a mass of undifferentiated units. If they were simply that, then "one man, one vote" would indeed be the sinister emblem of tyranny which it manifestly is in so many parts of the world. In a modern civilized state, the citizens are not a homogeneous mass of undifferentiated units—so many abstract statistics figuring in election returns. On the contrary, citizens organize themselves according to their various social, economic and political activities, in a multiplicity of groups and associations. It is the existence of these self-activated groups which gives vitality and power to the political institutions on which rests the legitimacy of government.

The idea that political legitimacy rests on popular sovereignty has had one consequence of particular importance. The sovereign people comprises the totality of the citizens. Citizens hold an immense variety of opinions and beliefs. Through long and bitter experience, from the onset of the Protestant Reformation onwards, it has come to be recognized that belief and opinion cannot serve as a criterion of citizenship, which must therefore be solely a matter of birth or choice. Thus, implicit in popular sovereignty is the idea of the secularity of the state—an idea now indispensable to good government and a free society.

These concepts and practices, taken as a whole, are what is understood by democracy in the West today. However, democracy is an ambiguous and equivocal word which can easily be exploited in double-talk, and which, taken on its own, is incapable of giving one an appreciation of the complex of ideas and institutions which serve as a specific against despotism and a safeguard for political freedom. It is safer, more exact, and more intelligible to speak rather of constitutional and representative government. Indeed, for our present purposes, this expression is preferred since if we look at the Arab world in modern times, its quest for democracy has in effect been a quest for constitutional and representative government.

This quest has a long history during the nineteenth and twentieth centuries. What is remarkable about it is that there is nothing in the political traditions of the Arab world—which are the political traditions of Islam— which might make familiar, or indeed intelligible, the organizing ideas of constitutional and representative government. The notion of a state as a specific territorial entity which is endowed with sovereignty, the notion of popular sovereignty as the foundation of governmental legitimacy, the idea of representation, of elections, of popular suffrage, of political institutions being regulated by laws laid down by a parliamentary assembly, of these laws being guarded and upheld by an independent judiciary, the ideas of the secularity of the state, of society being composed of a multitude of self-activating, autonomous groups and associations—all these are profoundly alien to the Muslim political tradition.

What, in brief, is this tradition? It is one which begins with the small community presided over by the Prophet Mohammed at Medina. This community, the *umma* of Muslims, has its *raison d'être* in Islam itself, in the revelation sent to the believers through the Prophet. What this revelation reveals is a divine plan for the salvation of those who hearken to the message, and who thus constitute the *umma*.

Wherever the Muslim *umma* is, there is the polity of Islam. Elsewhere is the abode of war. This, in a nutshell, is the Islamic theory of international relations. The abode of Islam, *dar-al-islam*, is not defined by permanent territorial frontiers. It is wherever Muslims exercise (or have exercised) dominion. *Dar-al-islam* is not like the Roman Empire, a city-state developing into an extensive Empire; it is unlike the Greek *polis*, or the state as it has developed in Europe. Its basis is neither kinship, nor the occupation of a defined territory, and the bond between its members is not legal, as in the Roman Empire, but religious: the members of the *umma* are such because they acknowledge the divine revelation as vouchsafed in the Koran, and obey its injunctions. The nearest analogy to the *umma* in Western terms is the *respublica christiana*. This *respublica*, however, never became a political reality.

The *umma*, on the other hand, was a reality from its beginnings in Medina, and even more so when the Muslims very quickly conquered the Middle East, Central Asia, parts of India as well as North Africa and large parts of the Iberian peninsula. This empire, as we would call it, was governed by a caliph, who was the successor to Mohammed as ruler, justiciar and military leader. In the political theory of Islam, as it has remained to the present day, the caliph is the sole political and military authority within the *umma*, and all civil officials and military officers are his servants and derive their powers solely from this, the highest public office in Islam. There can be no question of checks and balances, of division of power, of popular sovereignty, of elections or representative assemblies.

In its original form, Islamic political theory took for granted that the ruler would be a godly ruler, upholding the *Sharia*, and that his commitment to God's law gave sanction to his authority and constituted the bond between him and the other believers. However, fairly soon following the establishment of the Muslim empire, it became quite clear that any theoretical restraint which obedience to the *Sharia* might have imposed was of no consequence whatsoever. The ancient traditions of the Oriental despotism which had obtained in the newly conquered territories served immeasurably to magnify the position of the Muslim ruler, and it became more than ever out of the question for the subjects to bring to bear on the conduct of public officers their views and interests, even had there been institutions which might serve to articulate these views and interests.

The duty to obey the ruler, who was the Prophet's apostolic successor, was a religious duty, because the ruler maintained the religion, defended the territory in which it had become established, and enlarged its bounds. The subsequent vicissitudes of Muslim society, the civil wars which broke out periodically, the insubordinate soldiers and the disorders created by the ambitions of the military gave an unexpected (and lasting) twist to the theory that obedience to the caliph was a religious duty. In view of the perils to which the continuous disorders and the arbitrariness of military usurpers exposed the believers, the divines came to argue that passive obedience to any ruler who had hold of power, however he came by it, and whether he was bad or mad, was a religious duty. The reason for such an injunction is that anarchy is to be feared above all else, since anarchy makes impossible the pursuit of a godly life, and thus endangers eternal salvation which is the ultimate goal of all human endeavor. As the great divine Ghazali (d.1111) declared: "The tyranny of a sultan for a hundred years causes less damage than one year's tyranny exerted by the subjects against each other."

Traditional rule in the Middle East may be characterized as Oriental despotism in which, to use Karl Wittfogel's succinct description of this regime, the state is stronger than society. The reality of rule therefore marched together with the Islamic theory of politics as it came to be inculcated to the faithful, generation after generation. Such rule maintained, perforce, a great distance, not to say an outright separation, between concerns of the ruler and those of the ruled. The ruler's first concern is that there should be no challenge to his power and that as much wealth as possible should be squeezed out of the ruled to pay for his army and his court. Contrariwise, the main preoccupation of the ruled was to keep as low a profile as possible, to find ways of living with the exactions and the caprice of the ruler and his servants. Given this gulf between rulers and ruled, there could be no question of representative bodies being set up to carry on a dialogue between ruler and subject; neither could there be institutions of local self-government in town or countryside; nor could craft or professional associations flourish unhindered, since they would always be suspected of limiting the sway of the government over its subjects. In the nineteenth century, many Ottomans of the educated and official class were becoming increasingly familiar with European institutions and ideas, and eager to introduce them to their society. They sought to find equivalents in Islamic society for these institutions and ideas. One of them, a well-known writer, came up with a curious argument to the effect that in the past the Janissaries had been the equivalent of a popular representative body. As is well-known, the Janissaries were Ottoman slave-soldiers who constituted the most formidable military formation in the service of the sultans. However, from the seventeenth century onwards their discipline began to deteriorate considerably, and they became a kind of praetorian guard, given to periodical tumults and mutinies, and on occasion able to depose a sultan and set up another in his place. For the nineteenth century Ottoman writer, the disorderly corps of the Janissaries became spokesmen and representatives of the people, able to voice popular grievances and to act as a check on the ruler! This desperately fanciful argument is indication enough of the utter absence of traditions of self-government in the world of Islam.

As it happened, it was not European constitutionalism and representative government which first made an impact on the Middle East. It was rather another, and more recent, European outlook on government with which the Middle East initially became familiar and which Middle Eastern rulers attempted to apply. This outlook was articulated in the complex of ideas and institutions known as enlightened absolutism. This style of government became prevalent during the eighteenth century in many states in continental Europe, notably in Prussia, the Habsburg Empire and other German-speaking states, and in Russia. The style was based on the belief that there was a science of government which rulers could apply to increase the power of the state and the welfare of their subjects. The application of these ideas depended on an increasingly centralized bureaucracy through which the ruler sought to control economic activities as well as educational and social policies. Jeremy Bentham's celebrated *panopticon* may symbolize the character and ambitions of this new science of government. Bentham's *panopticon* was a design for a prison on scientific lines, in which the prisoners' cells were grouped around a central building from which the warders could have an uninterrupted view in all directions in order continuously to observe and control the behavior of the inmates, and thus to reform their characters and turn them into useful and virtuous citizens.

After Middle Eastern rulers began to feel the necessity of adopting European weapons and military techniques, it did not take long for them to realize that the European-style army required a European-style administration to back it up. The European-style of government which was most consonant with the traditional Oriental despotism was precisely that of enlightened absolutism. This style benefited, furthermore, from being associated with the military efficiency which Middle Eastern rulers were most anxious to acquire.

The first half of the nineteenth century thus saw in the Middle East a great increase in both bureaucracy and centralization, and an increase consequently in the readiness, and in the power, of governments to intervene in various social, economic and educational spheres which they had traditionally considered to be outside their purview. Since, again, the methods of the new-style bureaucracy were generally unfamiliar to the officials who now began to proliferate at the center and in the provinces, centralization became even more extreme leading to over-administration. The burden on the subject increased, while the gap widened between the universe of discourse common to traditional society and that of the Westernized functionaries, whereas previously rulers and subjects had shared common assumptions and common values.

Egypt under Mohammed Ali Pasha shows in a more extreme fashion than elsewhere in the Middle East—and thus more clearly—what kind of regime was replacing, under the impetus of modernization, the traditional despotism. Mohammed Ali was an Ottoman officer who came to Egypt with the troops sent to retake and garrison Egypt following Bonaparte's invasion in 1798. By 1805 he had managed to establish himself as the governor of this Ottoman province and set about systematically eliminating any opposition to his rule. With the help of European military officers and civilian advisers he created a formidable army on Westernized lines. To carry out an ambitious military and foreign policy which involved the conquest of the Sudan, expeditions to the Arabian Peninsula and to the Morea—in support of the Ottomans against the Greek rebellion—and the invasion of the Levant which bade fair at one point to lead to a catastrophic defeat of the Ottoman army, and the overthrow of the Ottoman dynasty, Mohammed Ali had to obtain the necessary resources, which could not but be considerable. He therefore laid his hands on practically all agricultural land in Egypt, of which he became the owner. He instituted a monopoly in the purchase and export of agricultural produce, and a monopoly likewise of imports and exports. He also set in train an ambitious industrialization programme in government-owned factories. The burden of his rapacity fell on all classes of the population, and people used to say that Mohammed Ali was jealous of the very fleas which fed on the fellah's blood.

I: Constitutionalist Experiments Before 1914

The traditions of Middle Eastern government, as has been seen, were not at all conducive to the introduction of constitutional and representative government. Furthermore, the character of the European ideas and institutions which were initially borrowed from Europe made it even more difficult and problematic for constitutionalist ideas to take root and prosper in the Middle East, the Arab world included.

However, with the passage of the years these ideas became more widely known among the educated and official class, and their attraction continued to increase. The reason for this was that the modernization on absolutist lines which had been attempted earlier was seen to be failing in its objective, which was to make these Middle Eastern states powerful and prosperous enough to be able to resist European encroachments. In fact, under modernization, military weakness seemed, if anything, to increase, while material prosperity was just as elusive. It was quite understandable, therefore, that it would be argued that mere military and administrative modernization was not the answer. The secret of European superiority, it was now believed, was not a matter of weapons and techniques. It was, rather, the outcome of the supremacy of the rule of law and the mutual checks and balances operating between elected legislatures and the executive.

Arguments in favor of constitutionalism carried conviction among the younger members of the Westernized official class. These arguments were also, no doubt, advanced by some out of ambition rather than conviction. Thus a prince from Mohammed Ali's dynasty, Mustafa

Fazil Pasha, brother of the ruler of Egypt, Ismail Pasha, disappointed in his political ambitions and living in Paris, addressed an open letter to the Ottoman Sultan in 1867 in which he attacked not the Sultan himself but the despotism of his officials. This despotism had practically destroyed all initiative on the part of the subjects. To prosper, citizens must have education, but education is not enough. What above all is required is liberty, as may be seen from the example of France, Italy, Prussia and Austria, and political liberty is assured through representative assemblies. Whether Mustafa Fazil himself really believed this is beside the point. What is of interest is that he thought it would be to his advantage, or to the disadvantage of his opponents, to hold this kind of language.

Among the countries which Mustafa Fazil held up as an example for the Sultan were two Arabic-speaking ones which were nominally part of the Ottoman Empire, but, to all intents and purposes, autonomous. These were Tunis and Egypt. In 1861, pressed by the representatives of France and Great Britain, and following a failed attempt to modernize militarily in imitation of Mohammed Ali, the Bey of Tunis granted his subjects a constitution. There was set up a Grand Council partly appointed by the Bey and partly co-opted. Ministers were supposed to be responsible to the Council whom the constitution also empowered to approve the enactment of new, and the amendment of old, laws. The Council also had oversight over both civil and military expenditures. What this constitution effected, however, was only a transference of autocratic powers from the Bey to the official class who controlled the administration, and who sat on the Council. Here was the facade of constitutionalism without its reality. What it meant for the ordinary subject was a vexatious increase in bureaucracy with the ways of which he was, anyway, unfamiliar, and a greater burden of taxes and of other disbursements intended to serve as sweeteners for office-holders. Under the old dispensation, officials were servants not of the public but of the ruler, and they used their offices in order to mulct those who had business with them of as much money as possible, in order to recoup what they might have had to pay the ruler for their offices, or to provide against impoverishment if they were to be suddenly deprived of their offices by the autocrat's whim. This did not change very much under the new dispensation, except that the number of officials who had to be squared had increased. The constitution, not unexpectedly, proved unpopular. Large areas of Tunis in the middle of the nineteenth century were tribal, and the central administration did not have the power or the resources to control them properly. When a tax—anyway unpopular—was raised, a rebellion broke out in protest not only against the tax, but also against the constitution as well. The constitution had to be suspended and remained so until the French imposed a protectorate in 1881.

The other Arabic-speaking country mentioned in Mustafa Fazil's open letter was Egypt, then being ruled by his brother Ismail. Ismail, a despot, had grandiose plans for the modernization of Egypt. At the opening of the Suez Canal in 1869 he proclaimed that the country would henceforth form part of Europe. Parliamentary institutions were clearly part of the civilization of Europe, and Ismail determined in 1868 that Egypt too should have a parliamentary assembly. It consisted of 75 members elected by village headmen. These headmen were, however, if not chosen, then certainly approved by the government. Ismail endowed his assembly with detailed regulations concerning debates, votes, etc., and he ordained that, as in all self-respecting assemblies, there should be two parties, one supporting, and the other opposing, the government. Members were understandably chary of being labelled as opponents of the government, and the ruler himself had to designate who should sit on the opposition benches.

The setting up of this assembly was obviously an empty gesture designed to show that Ismail was in tune with the spirit of the age. A decade or so later, when Ismail was in difficulties with foreign creditors, he imagined to use the assembly as a means of deflecting their pressure. The assembly, having been dormant for many years, was convoked and made to protest against exploitation and oppression by foreign bankers. No one was taken in by this gambit, and pressure by foreign powers, who had now become deeply involved in Egyptian affairs, led in 1879 to Ismail's deposition by his nominal suzerain, the Ottoman Sultan.

One of Ismail's strategies, a few years before his deposition, was to incite a mutiny by some Egyptian officers against a ministry which he had been forced to appoint, in order to bring some order into the public finances of Egypt, and find resources with which to repay the large debts Ismail had contracted. This action proved heavy with very serious consequences for Egypt. The officers, led by Colonel Orabi, had thus been taught to mutiny, and they proceeded to do so again on their own account after Ismail was succeeded by his son Tawfiq. They mutinied twice against him, in February and September 1881. Orabi set himself up as the spokesman of the downtrodden Egyptians, and an alliance was effected between the officers and members of the assembly designed to divest Tawfiq of his autocratic powers and make Egyptian government responsible to the representatives of the Egyptian people. This, however, was easier said than done. The members of the assembly, generally landowners, had been, in effect, chosen by the ruler, and it was very doubtful whether they were in any real sense the representatives of the Egyptian people. But even if they had been, power had passed not to them but to the Army colonels led by Orabi, now minister of defense, who had intimidated and cowed the ruler. It was not long before Orabi clashed with France and Great Britain who demanded his removal in May 1882. Tawfiq removed him, but Tawfiq's life was threatened by the colonels and Orabi was reinstated. The crisis led shortly afterwards to the bombardment of Alexandria by the British Navy, and to the British occupation of Egypt.

Orabi was captured, tried and banished to Ceylon. The Egyptian officers who had forced Tawfiq to submit to their will certainly resented the autocracy of the regime, as well as the ascendancy over them, who were native-born Eygptians, of what were called the Turco-Circassians who, like Mohammed Ali, had been Ottoman army officers, and who constituted the upper echelons of the Egyptian army. It may, however, be doubted whether an assembly such as that devised by Ismail could possibly have withstood the sway of a military cabal led by a forceful officer who had learnt how easy it was to impose his will on both ministers and rulers.

Aside from Tunis and Egypt, most of the rest of the Arabic-speaking countries were directly governed by the Ottomans, and their fate was bound up with developments in Istanbul, the Ottoman capital. At the same time as the events described above were unfolding in Egypt, the Ottoman Empire was experiencing a military crisis which in turn led to an attempt to establish parliamentary government—an attempt which was to have long-term repercussions in the Empire generally, including the Arab provinces. Nationalist disturbances in the Ottoman possessions in the Balkans led to a war with Russia which had intervened in support of its Slav co-religionists. In 1876, Russia was at the gates of Istanbul and a serious international crisis eventuated. At this juncture, some high Ottoman officials, military and civilian, became persuaded that drastic action was necessary to save the state. The most prominent and influential among them was a minister, Midhat Pasha, who had served as a governor in Baghdad and in the province of the Danube and had there earned a reputation as an efficient reformer. An anonymous manifesto distributed in Istanbul in March 1876, most probably by Midhat's followers, declared that if the country were ruled by a wise monarch supported by a consultative assembly in which the various races and religions were represented, it would without difficulty attain the prosperity to which it could aspire, given its resources and the resourcefulness of its population. Midhat, who became a minister without portfolio in a new ministry which took office in May 1876, organized together with the war minister and the director of the military academy a *coup d'état* in order to depose the reigning Sultan, with the acquiescence of the Grand Vizier, of the highest religious dignitary of the Empire, and various other high-ranking officers and officials. The conspirators replaced the deposed Sultan by a nephew believed to favor political reform. This was at the end of May. The new Sultan declared on his accession that he reigned "by the favor of the Almighty and the will of my subjects." The new Sultan, however, proved of unsound mind, and had to be deposed three months later. He was replaced by a brother, Abd al-Hamid, who gave assurances that he was as much in favor of a constitution as his brother.

The new Sultan was not a Tunisian Bey under the control of his officials. After his accession he stubbornly fought, and in the end defeated, attempts to promulgate a constitution which would transfer all power from himself to a prime minister presiding over a cabinet exercising collective responsibility. In the circumstances this would have simply meant that the Sultan's autocracy would have been replaced by the autocracy of the council of ministers. After lengthy negotiations between the Sultan and Midhat, who was now the Grand Vizier, a constitution was agreed and promulgated by the Sultan in December 1876.

The constitution provided for a senate and a chamber of deputies. The senate was to be wholly appointed by the Sultan, while the lower chamber was to be elected by members of the provincial and local councils—bodies which had been set up earlier in the century. The members of these councils were themselves indirectly elected, in a process which the authorities had ample means of influencing and controlling. It was to be expected that a parliament of this kind would obey the wishes either of the Sultan or of his ministers depending on which side was seen to be more powerful. The powers of the parliament were very limited. It could meet only when summoned by the Sultan, and was prorogued at his pleasure. It could not initiate legislation or modify existing laws. Members could vote only on bills submitted on behalf of the Sultan.

Only two parliaments were elected—one at the beginning and one at the end of 1877. The second was abruptly dissolved by the Sultan in February 1878. A year before, the Sultan had ordered Midhat seized and deported abroad. Midhat was allowed to return later and was appointed as governor first of Syria and then of Izmir. The Sultan, however, must have remained suspicious of Midhat, for he had him arrested while he was governor of Izmir, brought to Istanbul, and tried together with various of his confederates who had mounted the *coups d'état* of 1876 as a result of which Abd al-Hamid himself was now on the throne. They were accused of having plotted to kill Abd al-Hamid's uncle, Sultan Abd al-Aziz, who had indeed been found with his throat cut—it was said at the time that he had committed suicide—in the palace quarters to which he had been confined shortly after his deposition. Midhat was found guilty by the special court set up to try the accused, and sentenced to banishment at Taif in the Hijaz, where Abd al-Hamid had him killed in 1883.

Abd al-Hamid ruled from 1876 until his power was shattered by the military *coup d'état* organized by the Young Turks in July 1908 who, in another *coup d'état* in April 1909, deposed him and sent him into exile. Abd al-Hamid proved to be the last Ottoman Sultan to continue the tradition of administrative centralization in the cause of reform and modernization which his predecessors had initiated in the first decades of the nineteenth century. Just as the earlier bout of autocratic modernization had issued in discontent within the official and educated class and eventually led to Midhat's attempt to establish parliamentary government, so Abd al-Hamid's modernization, particularly of the army, itself conjured up increasing numbers of discontented officials and officers who came to believe that the ills of the Empire, the absence of public liberties at home and weakness abroad, were all to be laid at the door of the despot. The remedy for them, as it had been for Midhat, was the institution of parliamentary government, which Abd al-Hamid had nipped in the bud shortly after its establishment. A number of junior officers in the Third Army Corps stationed in Macedonia mutinied in July 1908 and demanded the reestablishment of the constitution of 1876. The Sultan, old and ill, and finding that other troops were joining the mutineers, gave way. The constitution was proclaimed anew, and elections held forthwith.

The officers, now the real rulers of the Empire, were organized in a Committee of Union and Progress which, with the success of the *coup d'état*, received many adherents and supporters and established branches in provincial centers. It was natural that the newly-elected deputies, as well as the provincial administration, should be responsive to the views and wishes of the new masters. It became speedily clear that the Sultan's autocracy now devolved on the leaders of the Committee. But quarrels and rivalries soon erupted among the officers, and it was the manner in which these quarrels were settled, not the outcome of the elections, which decided who should rule the Empire. By 1911 there was an open split among the officers, which was reflected in dissensions within the parliament. The faction in power became impatient and dissolved the chamber of deputies in January 1912. In the elections which followed, called, graphically, the "big stick" elections, all but six of the successful candidates were supporters of the administration. The following July a military *coup d'état* by dissident officers brought down the government, and installed one favorable to the new masters. The recently elected parliament was dissolved. In January 1913 Union and Progress officers led by Enver, one of the leaders of the 1908 coup, burst into the Sublime Porte—the headquarters of the government—where the council of ministers was meeting and forced their resignation at gunpoint, the Minister of War being shot dead during the fracas. This ensured, once and for all, the triumph of the Committee whose leaders remained the unchallenged masters of the state until they fled in ignominy in October 1918 when the world war which they had joined on the side of the Central Powers ended in the defeat and destruction of the Empire.

In retrospect both Midhat and the Young Turk officers (like Orabi in Egypt) may be seen as engaged in a paradoxical enterprise. They were convinced that autocracy was deeply harmful, that it caused economic backwardness and military weakness, and that it subjected the people to the corrupt and oppressive whims of the ruler and his servants. They believed that constitutionalism, representative government and the rule of law were the only remedies for their ruinous condition. The only way, unfortunately, to abolish autocracy was by means of conspiracy and *coup d'état*. However such methods themselves seemed inevitably only to substitute one kind of autocracy for another. The Arab world—in Egypt or in the Arab successor states of the Ottoman Empire—was subsequently to find itself caught in a paradox of this kind, namely that reform of corrupt and oppressive regimes by forcible means would itself end by creating the kind of regime escape from which in a legal and orderly manner is again impossible.

Middle Eastern modernization has also created another problem. In the traditional, despotic, order rulers and ruled shared a common universe of discourse. Their world-view was the same, they took for granted that government did not concern itself, or meddle with certain areas of private and social life like familial relations, education or the economy—provided of course that taxes were paid and the ruler's interests satisfied. With modernization there came to be a gap in outlook more or less wide, between the educated and official class, on the one hand, and the mass of the people on the other. The two sides increasingly spoke different languages from one another, and their assumptions and expectations concerning politics and political action diverged increasingly. A striking illustration of this divergence occurred during the events which led to Sultan Abd al-Hamid's deposition in April 1909. As will be recalled, the previous July Abd al-Hamid had been forced to reestablish the constitution by a *coup d'état* carried out by officers stationed in Salonika. This action seems to have led to great disgruntlement on the part of army units stationed in Istanbul. These units rose up against the *coup d'état*, and called upon the Sultan to do away with the changes which he had been forced to make under the pressure of these mutinous officers. It is interesting and significant that the officers of these units had risen from the ranks and thus had not been exposed to the westernizing influence which their Salonika counterparts had imbibed in the military colleges which Abd al-Hamid's zeal for military modernization caused him to establish in various provinces. The Salonika officers were sure that Abd al-Hamid was behind the uprising in the capital, and proceeded to march on Istanbul and depose him. Afterwards the commander of the Salonika contingent confessed that he did not divulge the real purpose of the expedition lest the troops refuse to obey. He told them that they were going to Istanbul in order to defend the Sultan.

This gap between the westernized official classes and the mass had consequences for the representativeness of representative institutions when these were attempted to be set up. In the traditional regime where these institutions did not exist, but where ruler and ruled shared a common universe of discourse, there was, it may be argued, a considerable element of informal representativeness present. Notables, tribal leaders, divines, heads of non-Muslim communities, had access to rulers and their officials, could bring grievances to their notice and seek alleviations or remedies. The new European-style representative institutions were very remote from the population, which was unfamiliar with the idea of votes and elections, and which had little access to the members of an assembly. A member, furthermore, may have been elected, in a manner of speaking, for a large constituency, usually by the indirect mode, and may have often been the choice of a minister in the capital, or of the governor of the province. At any rate, he would probably not have the local standing or the local knowledge which used to make informal representativeness a valuable, albeit uncodified, element of governance. Even before country-wide parliamentary assemblies were created, the experience of local councils, set up to promote local self-government in the Ottoman Empire, had proved quite dismal. They became simply yet another layer of the new-fangled bureaucracy. Their workings, quite unfamiliar to the population they were supposed to benefit, became yet another means whereby those who knew the ins and outs of the European-style system could manipulate it to their profit. Sooner or later, the central government became aware of the ill-success of these local bodies, and more than once tinkered with them, in an attempt to make them work as they were meant to, but to no avail. It may be added that local government bodies such as municipalities which could be considered as local in any genuine sense, and not as emanations or agencies of the central government, have, in the Arab world, uniformly failed to take.

II: Iraq, 1921-1938

 The political tradition of Islam, and the European-style modernization which large parts of the Middle East increasingly experienced in the century between the Congress of Vienna and the outbreak of the World War in 1914, left their indelible mark on what may be called Arab political culture. As has been seen, neither the Islamic tradition, nor the European enlightened absolutism which was adopted by modernizing rulers and officials, was conducive to the introduction and development of constitutional and representative government.

The World War and its aftermath had manifold drastic and lasting consequences for the Middle East, and for the Arab world in particular—consequences which are still felt to the present day. It is no exaggeration to say that the war destroyed whatever remained of the traditional order and the loyalties it had fostered which had survived the forceful attempts at military and administrative modernization. The war, again, for the first time in the modern world, put the Arabs on the stage of politics. During the war, the British, seeking ways of dealing with the Ottomans who had joined their enemies, entered into secret negotiations with Hussein, the Sharif of Mecca, a Young Turk appointee who later fell out with the Istanbul government and sought, just before the war, to inveigle the British into supporting him. In June 1916, Hussein unexpectedly declared rebellion against the Ottomans, even though his negotiations with the British had been inconclusive, and he had obtained no hard-and-fast undertaking from them. In his negotiations, Hussein sought the establishment of a far-flung Arab state which, he claimed, was the object of a wide conspiracy by Arab officers in the Ottoman army who would, if the British agreed to their demands, rise in rebellion against the Ottomans and paralyze Ottoman power, at the very least in Syria.

This prospect proved illusory, but Hussein became the standard-bearer of Arabism. He proclaimed himself King of the Arab Countries, though the utmost the Allies agreed to was to recognize him as King of the Hijaz. This, however, was the beginning of the claim that the Arabs constituted a nation and ought, therefore, to form an independent state. It was also thus the beginning of a long process leading eventually to a transvaluation of values. Those who had hitherto identified themselves as Muslims, albeit of Arab speech, their loyalty going to the Sultan-Caliph, now gradually learned to look upon themselves as Arabs first and foremost, members of the Arab nation upholding the abiding values of Arabism. It is only at this stage that one may begin to speak of Arab politics and Arab political culture.

The Western Powers who destroyed the Ottoman Empire during 1914-18 were to impinge with great force on the Arabic-speaking areas of the Ottoman Empire. These areas were detached from the Empire and were constituted by the newly-formed League of Nations into "mandates." The theory of the mandates as enunciated by President Woodrow Wilson, and later included in the League Covenant, was to the effect that areas which had formed part of the defeated Empires, and chiefly the Ottoman Empire, were not ready for self-government. They were to be prepared for it by mandatory powers who would guide their first steps and save them from stumbling. Eventually, as the theory had it, the mandated territories would become ready for self-government, whereupon the mandatory powers would lay down their responsibilities and retire from the scene.

This high-minded doctrine was, however, too good for this world. What in fact happened was that the two Great Powers who had emerged victorious became the mandatories of those ex-Ottoman territories where they had interests, and upon the disposal of which they had secretly agreed in the course of the war. Thus, Britain became the mandatory for Iraq and Palestine, and France for Syria and the Lebanon.

It has to be said, however, that mandates were not a mere charade. Both mandatories set up, in the territories for which they were responsible, representative parliamentary institutions. This was not only to conform to the requirements of the mandate, but also because the mandatory governments themselves believed that the territories where they exercised responsibility for the time being should have constitutions and representative rule. The local governments which they set up also believed that this was a feature of modern civilization which they should acquire.

The mandate for Palestine, entrusted to Britain, was similar to the other mandates in that it charged the mandatory with promoting institutions of self-government; however, unlike the other mandates, it incorporated in its preamble the language of the Balfour Declaration which spoke of viewing with favor the establishment of a Jewish national home in Palestine. Hence, the Palestine mandate also required the mandatory to promote the establishment of such a national home. However, it soon appeared that this additional requirement cut across the other one. As was seen in the 1920s and 1930s, attempts by the mandatory to set up a representative assembly fell foul either of Arab or of Zionist opposition. Thus, so long as the mandate lasted, i.e. until May 15, 1948 when the British evacuated the territory, leaving it prey to disorder and war, Palestine was governed by a High Commissioner answerable only to the Colonial Office in London.

Matters were very different in the other British mandate, Iraq. The territory of this mandate comprised three ex-Ottoman provinces, Mosul, Baghdad and Basra. That these three quite different provinces, which had previously never been grouped together, were now to form a single state was entirely due to the fact that by the end of the war they had been conquered by the British, who had laid claim to them in negotiations with their wartime allies.

The British claim to these three provinces was ratified by a decision of the Allies, in April 1920, to assign to Britain the mandate for the area. The three provinces were now grouped in a new state, called Iraq, for which brand-new political and administrative arrangements would have to be made. In the event, the British set up a kingdom, with its capital in Baghdad, to be ruled by a king which they imported from outside.

This new king was Faisal, third son of the King of the Hijaz whom they had previously installed in Damascus when Allenby conquered it at the beginning of October 1918. Damascus, Aleppo and their hinterland, conquered by British forces, were allowed to be taken over by Faisal in an attempt to foil the French who, according to wartime agreements, were to be predominant in this territory. A year later, the British abandoned this strategy and left Faisal to deal with the French on his own. A clash between them soon ensued, the French occupied Damascus and expelled Faisal and his followers in July 1920. Faisal had friends in London, notably Colonel T. E. Lawrence, now an official in the Colonial Office where he had the ear of the Colonial Secretary, Winston Churchill. Lawrence represented that Faisal had been unfairly treated and should be compensated by being given the throne of the new state of Iraq. This had, furthermore, the advantage of relieving the British of worry and expense in administering their mandate, since Faisal would use his position to ensure orderly and peaceful conditions.

Churchill agreed, and a plebiscite was engineered which showed the usual overwhelming majority in favor of the British-sponsored candidate. In due course, a constitutional assembly was set up which drafted a constitution and an electoral law, and made provision for a parliament. In 1930, some ten years after the beginning of the mandate, Britain announced that Iraq was now fully ready for self-government and asked the League of Nations to admit it as a fully-fledged sovereign state. However, soon after the termination of the British mandate in 1932, it became clear that constitutional and parliamentary government had little or no chance of functioning in Iraq. The reasons were inherent in the very character of the kingdom invented and set up by the British. As has been stated, the new state consisted of three ex-Ottoman provinces. These provinces were very different from one another and had never been governed as one entity on its own. The northernmost province, Mosul, had a predominance of Kurds and Turks, though Mosul City, the provincial capital, was predominantly Arab. The province of Baghdad, to the south, was predominantly Arab Sunni, though its capital, Baghdad City, had a mixed population of Sunnis, Shi'a and Jews, all Arabic-speaking; none of these had a majority, but the Jews—the oldest group with a continuous record of living in Mesopotamia—formed the largest group. To the south of Baghdad, the extensive area of the Middle and Lower Euphrates was predominantly Shi'i, though the provincial capital of Basra, the City (and port) of Basra, was largely Sunni. Furthermore, the largest part of the population, whether Arab or Kurdish, was tribal, whether composed of nomads or semi-nomads, or settled fellahin. It was illiterate, unable to understand unfamiliar concepts such as elections and parliamentary representation, and accustomed to obey their tribal leaders and such government officials as came into contact with them and, in the case of the Shi'a, also revering the religious divines residing in Najaf, Karbala and other shrine cities in Iraq sacred to the Shi'i world.

More than half of this extremely heterogeneous population was Shi'i and about a fifth was Kurdish. Faisal, a Sunni, and his predominantly Sunni administration, thus were given the power to rule over a population in its overwhelming majority neither Sunni nor Arab.

Other events preceding Faisal's coming also cast their long shadow over the prospects of constitutional, parliamentary government in Iraq. The major reason that Churchill wanted Faisal to be the King of Iraq was an insurrection in the Euphrates by Shi'i tribesmen in the summer of 1920. The insurrection was the outcome of resentment by some tribal chiefs over the way in which the British civil administration had favored some of their rivals, and of the political ambition of the Shi'i divines who had been politicized—and radicalized—by the role they had played before the war in challenging the Shah's autocracy in Persia. The fact that after the end of the war the British occupiers seemed unclear which policy to follow in Iraq led these divines to hope that, given the Shi'i majority, they stood a good chance of controlling any state which would succeed the occupation, and they sought to establish their claim by inciting an insurrection. They were encouraged in their dreams by emissaries from Faisal's regime in Damascus. These emissaries represented Sunni ex-Ottoman officers who hailed from Baghdad or Mosul, who had deserted to the Sharif of Mecca and who had official positions in Faisal's regime (supported, financed and armed by the British). They did not see why they should not also rule in the areas from which they themselves originated.

Though they were taken by surprise to start with, the British defeated the insurrection within a few months, and thus ended the dreams of a Shi'i-dominated state. However, shortly afterwards, the British brought in Faisal, accompanied by the very officers who had helped spark the rebellion against them. Instead of being punished for their complicity, they were, as it seemed to the Shi'i leaders, handsomely rewarded, and given power to keep down the Shi'a as Sunni governments had done for centuries. So from the very outset, the leaders and spokesmen of the Shi'a harbored a deep resentment against the new state. This resentment created a deep and lasting rift within the body politic, making it very difficult, not to say impossible, for any sense of common purpose or of mutual loyalty to exist between the small number of Sunni officials and officers, who in effect constituted the state, and the mass of the Shi'a, who were not so much citizens as subjects. The same is true for the Kurds, who had never before been ruled from Baghdad, and refused to acquiesce in Arab rule over them, to which, again, they had never before been subjected. The newly-invented polity was thus fragmented and fractured from the very beginning. The original fault-lines have become, if anything, more pronounced with every change of regime. The Kurdish and Shi'i uprisings in the aftermath of the Iraqi defeat at the hands of the U.S. in 1991 eloquently show the abiding disaffection of the majority of the population towards rule from Baghdad.

Another characteristic of the new state also boded ill for the prospects of constitutional government. The ex-Ottoman officers who came with Faisal and became the pillars of the monarchy had imbibed from the Young Turk officers who had been their contemporaries and colleagues a readiness to engage in violence and conspiracy in pursuit of political aims. Desertion from the army to which they had sworn allegiance—a very serious step for an officer— must have encouraged these proclivities. To take as example an early incident which took place when the mandate was still in being, the Baghdad-born Nuri ibn Said (known to his Baghdadi fellows as ibn al-mallata, son of the wet-nurse), had deserted in 1914 while a lieutenant. Ten years later, General Nuri al-Said (having in the meantime added the honorific 'al' to his name to give the impression that he was descended from an old and illustrious family) was head of the police in Iraq. A member of the constituent assembly was suspected of harboring republican sentiments which might harm

Faisal's standing; Nuri thereupon arranged for him to be rubbed out.

Even before the mandate ended it was becoming clear that this deeply fractured polity delivered into the hands of a foreigner, ruling by means of a handful of Sunni officers and officials, could not, parliament or no parliament, be governed constitutionally or within the rule of law. Elections were the outcome not of voters' choice, but rather of the wishes of the government acting through its administrative officials. This was what might be expected given that the electorate was generally illiterate, that the officials could exert great power and, as the administration became better established and assumed an increasing range of functions, attained greatly increasing power. Between 1925, when the first parliament was elected, and May 1958, when the last elections took place, less than two months before the destruction of the monarchical regime, a total of 16 parliaments were returned. All of them conformed to the wishes of the government for the time being in power. To start with, elections were indirect. In 1952, however, following riots in Baghdad, the government then in office resigned, and the chief of staff was appointed prime minister; he, presumably as a measure of appeasement, made elections direct. This, however, in no way changed the outcome of elections which followed. In the very last elections, in May 1958, in 116 constituencies out of 148 there was a single candidate and thus no voting was necessary.

Changes of government therefore were not the outcome of, say, changing parliamentary majorities, but of in-fighting among the small number of ministers and would-be ministers who followed one another with great rapidity in the Baghdad merry-go-round. Between 1921 when Faisal I was proclaimed King and 1958 when his young grandson and successor was mowed down by officers of his army, 58 cabinets followed one another. In these short-lived administrations no more than some 175 ministers enjoyed the profits of office. Most of these were obscure and ephemeral figures, hangers-on, opportunists on the make and parasitic followers dependent on the favor of the royal court and the handful of bosses—Nuri, Yasin al-Hashimi, Rashid Ali, etc.,—who were the principal orchestrators of these political games. Patrons and clients disappeared without trace when the monarchy was destroyed in 1958.

For all its power over the population at large, the monarchical regime was, then, very narrowly based, and its principal players insecure. For they had no public loyalties on which to rely, and none of that public support which, in constitutional governments, gives authority and self-confidence to an elected leader. In the small, dangerous cockpit of the capital they had to conduct their fights— more or less ruthless and sometimes bloody—against rivals perpetually plotting to have the better of them.

Between 1932 and 1936 one weapon which power-seekers in Baghdad used was to incite tribal leaders in the Euphrates to rise up against the government. Time and again the strategy worked, governments were toppled and their rivals succeeded them and proceeded to reward their tribal confederates. In attempting to put down these uprisings, governments had recourse to the army. Sooner rather than later, army commanders came to wonder why they should exert themselves on behalf of the Baghdad politicians, when they could act on their own with great profit to themselves. Thus a cycle of military *coups d'état* began in 1936 which went on until 1941. During this period governments in Baghdad changed at the whim of the army officers.

The last *coup d'état* in this particular cycle occurred in April 1941. Because it took place during the war, and because the four colonels who organized it had pro-Nazi sympathies and tried to get German support against the British whom they hated as the oppressors of Iraq and the patrons of Zionism, the British took this *coup d'état* very seriously since it threatened to turn Iraq into a German base, and they hastened to intervene and nip the movement in the bud. Their security required that they should be fully in control of Iraq lest the Germans should again have an opportunity to implant themselves in this strategically crucial area. Between 1941 and 1945, then, the British were the ultimate arbiters. They purged the army and the civil service of anyone suspected of pro-Nazi anti-British sympathies, and their views decided the make-up of the cabinets.

After 1945, when British control was relaxed, Iraqi politics remained very much the preserve of the narrow group which had dominated it before. The army purge ensured that for a period of time, at least, the officers would not intervene in politics. But other elements appeared which served to increase, on the one hand, the power and influence of the court, and on the other the fragility of the regime. In order to guard against the ambition of politicians who might be tempted to use the army, or any other element, to advance their ambitions, the monarch was given power to dismiss ministers at his discretion. This meant a further concentration and centralization of power, making constitutional and representative government even more of a mockery than before.

A new political volatility became apparent, however, which made governments more fearful and thus more prone to be heavy-handed in suppressing anything which might seem to threaten them. This volatility was due to the spread among the young of ideologies such as communism and pan-Arabism—a spread which went hand in hand with the increase in numbers of graduates from high schools and colleges where they were politicized by teachers committed to this or that ideology. The diffusion of these ideologies resulted in demonstrations and riots led by fairly well-organized activists. Such riots took place in 1946, 1948 and 1952 and on the last two occasions they resulted in the fall of the government. However, it was not these public commotions which brought about the downfall of the monarchical regime, all its institutions and the political figures who, during its brief span, benefited from it to satiation.

A military *coup d'état* was responsible, for in spite of the large network of informers and spies within the armed forces, the government and the court were caught unawares when the fatal hour arrived at dawn on July 14, 1958. In the decades which followed and which saw commotion after commotion in Iraq, none of those who played a role in its murderous politics seriously thought of constitutional representative government as an option.

III: Syria, 1928-1949

The country known today as Syria consists of the largest part of the Ottoman province of Aleppo and of parts of the province of Damascus, and of the northernmost bit of the province of Beirut. Its boundaries were fixed more or less by the Anglo-French Asia Minor Agreement of May 1916, and by French decisions after the war. Like Iraq, Syria became a mandated territory, and the mandate was assigned to France. Unlike Iraq, Syria has a Sunni majority, but the northwest includes a compact Alawite minority, while the south and southeast has an equally compact Druze population, also a minority. As in Iraq, however, the ex-Ottoman provinces which made up the Syrian state had never been governed as a distinct entity on their own, and there were many differences between the two provinces of Aleppo and Damascus in the outlook of their inhabitants and in their economic orientation. The province of Aleppo in its economic activity looked towards the Mediterranean, having its outlet on the sea at the port of Tripoli, which the French in 1920 included in the new Lebanese state, also towards Mosul to the east and Anatolia and Cilicia to the north and northeast. Aleppo City, the capital of the province, was an important commercial entrepot and a cosmopolitan center with a mixed population of Arabs, Turks, Armenians, Jews, Kurds, and long-established European traders.

Damascus, on the other hand, looked toward the desert, east, south and southeast. The province contained a sizeable bedouin population, and it had old-established links, through its commerce and its bedouin population, with the Hijaz and Najd. The pilgrimage caravans started from its capital city, Damascus, which was overwhelmingly Arab and Sunni. The Hijaz railway, built by Sultan Abd al-Hamid with subscriptions contributed by the whole Muslim world, and the purpose of which was politico-religious as well as military, began in Damascus.

The new state of Syria, then, with its two very different regions, each of which included important non-Sunni populations was, as the mandate required, to be inducted into self-government. In trying to discharge this obligation, the French mandatory followed a sensibly different policy from the British in Iraq. Article 1 of the mandate declared that the mandatory "shall, as far as circumstances permit, encourage local autonomy." In Iraq, the British conspicuously neglected any provision for local autonomy, establishing a tightly centralized state, even though the highly heterogeneous character of the country cried out for the provision of local autonomy. Not only did the British not provide for such autonomy, they also actively discouraged demands for it. The Assyrian Christian community, fearful of being oppressed by a Muslim government in Baghdad, repeatedly asked that its communal autonomy be established before the end of the mandate, but the British, who used the Assyrians as local levies to guard their airfield installations, cold-shouldered and rebuffed them. The Kurds, likewise, received no encouragement in their requests for a measure of regional self-government. When the League of Nations terminated the mandate for Iraq, it stipulated that the Kurds along with the other minorities should be enabled to preserve their language and culture and that Kurds should take a prominent part in the administration of Kurdish areas—a stipulation which Iraq initially accepted, but utterly disregarded after its sovereignty was recognized. The British government, in its character of former mandatory, as well as of a member of the League, had a certain responsibility to see that the stipulation should not be so cavalierly neglected, but in fact it made not the slightest attempt to raise the issue, either with the Iraqi government or at Geneva.

The French proceeded very differently in Syria. They established separate states in Damascus, in Aleppo and in the Druze country, and provided for a separately governed Alawite territory. Such a policy conformed to the realities of the country, which is not to say that it did not chime in with French interests. As will be recalled, in 1920 the French had clashed with Faisal and his Arab Sunni followers. They were concerned with guarding against the hostility of the Arab Sunnis in Syria. To this end, they set up a system of checks and balances, which recognized regional and sectarian interests, and which tried to ensure that such particularisms were not swamped or overwhelmed by an over-mighty center.

The League of Nations required the mandatory to frame a constitution within three years of the mandate coming into force. The Syrian mandate came into force in 1922. However, in 1925 serious disturbances broke out among the Druze and spread to other parts of the country. The Ottomans had never found it easy to rule the Druze areas, and the period from October 1918 to July 1920, when Faisal's government was nominally in control, weakened further the power of the central government over this warlike population which was accustomed to obey its own leaders rather than officials appointed by a remote and unfamiliar authority. The French proved heavy-handed and maladroit in asserting their presence, and aroused fears among the Druze chieftains that they were out to diminish them and erode their traditional position. It came to an armed clash. The French were caught in an ambush and sustained heavy losses in men and arms. This Druze success stoked the flames of insurrection, and had immediate repercussions elsewhere in Syria.

Political figures in Damascus had never reconciled themselves to the disappearance of the Arab government, and they now tried to give another complexion to what had been a local, tribal uprising. One of these Damascene figures established contact with the leader of the rebellion, Sultan al-Atrash. They agreed to proclaim a Syrian National Government headed by none other than the Sultan. There could be very little reality to a Syrian government headed by a Druze chieftain, even assuming that the French were totally eliminated from Syria. However, Druze fighters infiltrated into parts of Damascus on three occasions, there was a short-lived uprising in Hama, north of Damascus, and disorders in Aleppo. All of this hurt French prestige and delayed the drafting and promulgation of a constitution.

However, by early 1927 the troubles had died down and the mandatory thought it safe to take in hand the issue of the constitution. A constituent assembly was elected and it met in June 1928. The clear majority in this assembly was unpolitical and acquiescent in the wishes of the authorities. However, city notables with a local urban following were able to win many seats, and these members acted as an organized group. They were thus in a position to dominate the majority and push for their own views. The High Commissioner had left the drafting of the constitution to the assembly, and under the influence of the nationalist members, articles were included giving the Syrian government control over foreign policy and the army, and declaring that Lebanon and Palestine were part of Syria. This clearly went against the terms of the mandate, but the assembly would not, in response to the French High Commissioner's request, drop these provisions. Eventually the High Commissioner dissolved the assembly and promulgated the constitution by decree, minus the unacceptable clauses.

This episode is very instructive. For the nationalist members—who shortly afterwards formed a political party, the National Bloc—the purpose of being in the assembly was not to participate in the orderly processes of parliamentary government, and thus to share in the governance of the country, but to defy and discommode the mandatory through belligerent and spectacular gestures, with the object precisely of making parliamentary government impossible. The National Bloc used the same tactic in the parliament elected in 1932. In these elections there was, again, a non-nationalist majority in spite of disorders and intimidation fomented by the Bloc. By then the mandatory had decided to follow the British example in Iraq, and terminate the mandate. To this end the French proposed a draft treaty which would provide for a Syrian-French alliance—similar to the alliance the British had negotiated with Iraq preparatory to the termination of the mandate—and the admission of Syria to the League of Nations. The draft treaty, however, provided that the Druze and Alawite region should remain, for the time being at any rate, separate from the Syrian republic. The ministers appointed following the 1932 elections approved the draft, and the prime minister signed it. The Bloc thereupon organized demonstrations and riots in Damascus and other cities which led the High Commissioner to decide that the draft treaty could not be properly debated in the assembly, and he withdrew it from consideration. He also suspended the assembly, and in the face of continuous agitation and rioting, prorogued it indefinitely in November 1934. Here again, the purpose of the Bloc was to make unworkable parliamentary government, and in this they succeeded.

A year later, the obsequies of a well-known nationalist leader were made the occasion for renewing the agitation for a unitary and centralized Syrian state in which Druze, Alawites and Turks in the province of Alexandretta—which remained part of the Syrian mandate until the French ceded it to Turkey in 1938—and Kurds in the northeastern Jazira plain would all be ruled from Damascus by what would inevitably be an Arab Sunni government. The High Commissioner would not give way to the agitation. However, a new French left-of-center government in Paris decided that negotiations for a treaty should open with a Syrian delegation in Paris. The members of the delegation came predominantly from the Bloc, who claimed that they represented the Syrian people. There had, of course, been no electoral test to establish the extent of the Bloc's representativeness. The willingness of the French government to allow the Bloc a quasi-monopoly in negotiation lent a (spurious) credibility to the Bloc's exclusive claim of representativeness.

Negotiations with the Bloc, which in the event were conducted by the leftist Popular Front government, were quickly concluded, because the new French government conceded the principal demand of the Bloc leaders, namely that an independent Syria (which would come into being after three years) should be a centralized state ruled from Damascus. The triumph of the Bloc, and the clear evidence that the mandatory had given in to them, meant that they swept in to victory in the elections of November 1936. This electoral victory notwithstanding, the claim that the Bloc was the sole legitimate representative of the Syrian people, could not, in the event, be sustained.

The Bloc formed a government following their electoral victory, and ruled Syria—of course still under mandatory supervision—until July 1939. Bloc rule aroused a great deal of discontent. It was accused of nepotism and corruption, and of appointing its followers to the chief administrative posts in Druze and Alawite areas and in the Jazira. In power, the Bloc showed itself to be not what its name implied, i.e. a disciplined party, but rather a collection of notables with divergent and discordant interests, the most discordant being the interests of the Damascenes and those of the Aleppines. Bloc rule, again, was accompanied by a great deal of public disorder.

In imitation of what was being done in some European countries, the Bloc established a paramilitary organization, the Steel Shirts, in order to intimidate rivals and opponents. There followed clashes and brawls with similar organizations formed by rivals and opponents. These the Bloc could not suppress since the continuing presence of mandatory controls meant that the government was not at liberty, and did not have the power—like its fully sovereign successors in later years—to silence and suppress opposition.

The treaty which was triumphantly negotiated in 1936 eventually came to nothing because the Popular Front government fell in 1937, and its successors did not feel committed to the treaty which, anyway, aroused many misgivings and much opposition in the National Assembly. The international tension in Europe, the increasing imminence of war, the manifest incompetence of the Bloc in government and its maladministration—all this led the High Commissioner to suspend the constitution, dissolve the assembly, and appoint civil servants to run the various government departments. This state of affairs continued until after the fall of France in May 1940 and the establishment of the Vichy government, to which French civil and military authorities in the Levant declared their allegiance.

In the summer of 1941 Syria and the Lebanon were invaded by the British, seconded by a small Free French contingent. The invasion occurred because the British were afraid that Vichy would allow the Axis Powers to implant themselves in the Levant, and thus further threaten the Allied position in the Middle East—a position made already parlous enough by the fall of Greece and the presence of Axis forces in Cyrenaica and Tripoli.

Following the defeat of the Vichy forces and the expulsion of the Vichy officials, the Free French under de Gaulle took over the administration of what was still, despite the demise of the League of Nations, formally a French mandate. The reality however was that the preponderating power in the Levant was exercised by the British who, with their troops far exceeding in number the forces at de Gaulle's disposal, in effect garrisoned the area, and inevitably had a very large say in practically all aspects of its administration. On the eve of the invasion the British had pressed the Free French—in effect compelled them—formally to announce the independence of Syria (and of the Lebanon), in the belief that this would attract Arab support for the Allies, and also increase British popularity in the Middle East as a whole. The British followed up this pressure by also pressing for elections. The very dangerous threat posed to Egypt by Rommel in 1942, and the urgent need to deal with it, for a time lessened this pressure. With the Axis threat removed by the victory of Alamein, the pressure for elections resumed, and they were held in July 1943.

Like the elections of 1936, those of 1943 resulted in a landslide for the Bloc—and for similar reasons. By its success in negotiations with the French in 1936, the Bloc was establishing that it was the dominant element in Syrian politics, as the mandatory itself recognized, and elections merely ratified a prior triumph achieved in Paris. In 1943, likewise, since the Free French were compelled by British pressure to authorize elections, since the British—now dominant in the Middle East—were known to be sympathetic to the Bloc, and since the Bloc had always stood for the termination of the mandate, its electoral victory was a foregone conclusion.

The defeat of the Free French in their duel with the British effectively meant the end of the mandate and the attainment of full independence by the Syrian Republic. Between then and 1949, the notables of the Bloc split into two factions which reflected the rivalry, based on the divergent interests and the lack of any traditional political bonds, between Damascus and Aleppo. The Damascene faction called itself the National Party and the Aleppine one the People's Party. It was the National Party which continued to hold power, before and after new elections which took place in 1947. The majority of the deputies in the new assembly called themselves Independents, i.e. they were open to bids, pressures and manipulation by the government which was master of the country-wide administrative network and the considerable patronage which naturally went with it.

Such a state of affairs meant that a government in power could not be dislodged by ordinary electoral or parliamentary means, and that assemblies, which were representative in no intelligible sense, were the creatures rather than the masters of the government. Thus, the constitution prescribed that the President of the Republic would hold office for a single non-renewable term. The President wished to enjoy office for another term, and the assembly promptly complied by changing the constitution accordingly, and the President was elected for a second term in April 1948.

Unfortunately for him, the President was not able to enjoy his second term to its full extent. In March 1949 the Army Chief of Staff, disgruntled with the President and his ministers after the defeat of the Syrian forces in the Palestine war which had broken out in May 1948, organized a *coup d'état* which removed the President and his Prime Minister from office. A popular referendum in June elected him President. In August, he was toppled by another officer who had him executed. This officer was in turn toppled by a fellow-officer the following December. The three *coups d'état* of 1949 were the prelude to successive, albeit spasmodic, interventions by army officers which put paid, until this day, to any possibility of Syria being governed through parliamentary and representative institutions.

IV: Lebanon, 1926-1975

The French were assigned an additional mandate over another ex-Ottoman territory, which came to be known as the Republic of Lebanon. Just as Iraq and Syria each comprised Ottoman provinces which had never formed a political unit on their own, similarly the territories of the Lebanese Republic, within the frontiers laid down by the mandatory, had never been governed as one political unit with its own separate institutions. There had been between 1861 and 1915 an autonomous province of Mount Lebanon, but its territory was considerably smaller than the Republic of Lebanon which was formed in 1920.

This autonomous province did not include the area of Tripoli in the north, the areas of Sidon and Tyre in the south, or the Bekaa valley in the east, and it did not include the city of Beirut, which was now to become the capital of the new Republic. The autonomous province had consisted only of the—much smaller—territory of Mount Lebanon. This smaller territory was inhabited by Maronite Christians who predominated numerically, and by Druze, an esoteric sect stemming from Islam, whose members were much smaller than those of the Maronites, but whose political weight was much greater than their size, chiefly owing to their warlike proclivities.

The autonomous province of Mount Lebanon came into being following a time of troubles in the Mountain which lasted for two decades, culminating in a horrific massacre of large numbers of Maronites by Druze. The time of troubles came upon the Mountain following the Egyptian occupation of the Levant in the 1830s. During this period, Bashir, the Maronite ruler of the Mountain, sided with the Egyptians who used him to disarm the Druze and conscript both Maronites and Druze into Egyptian service. When Mohammed Ali was forced by the Powers to evacuate the

Levant, Bashir lost his position and was taken by the British to Malta as a prisoner. The Ottoman government took the opportunity of Bashir's downfall to try to control the Mountain and to put it under greater centralized rule than had ever been the case. Before then, the rulers of the Mountain had in effect been Ottoman feudatories who gave allegiance to the Sultan, in token of which they annually remitted taxes to Istanbul. The mountainous character of the territory and the warlike habits particularly of the Druze meant that the Ottomans were unable to exercise there the same sway as in other provinces, hence this feudal arrangement. The rulers of the Mountain—Druze in the sixteenth and seventeenth centuries, and Sunnis who converted to Maronite Catholicism, until Bashir's downfall—were themselves at the apex of a feudal hierarchy, reminiscent of West European feudalism. During the long centuries when this feudal system operated, Druze and Maronites had managed to establish among themselves a kind of coexistence.

This history has to be borne in mind when considering the institutions set up in the autonomous province of Mount Lebanon in 1861. The massacres of 1860 led the French to send an expeditionary force to Beirut with the object of protecting the Maronites. The other European Great Powers could not allow the French to act on their own, and the outcome was agreement over a constitution which would on the one hand insulate the Mountain from direct interference by the Ottoman government—an interference believed to have been mischievous in its consequences in the two previous decades, and on the other provide security for the two principal communities that neither would be able to oppress the other or disregard its interests. To this end it was agreed that the governor of the autonomous province would be a non-Lebanese Christian Ottoman subject. He would be appointed by the Ottoman government after consultation with the Powers who had, so to speak, brokered the settlement and would supervise and guarantee its orderly application.

To assist the governor in the discharge of his duties, there was set up an administrative council consisting of twelve members. Two were Maronites, two Druze, two Greek Catholic, two Greek Orthodox, two Sunnis and two Shi'a. The members of the council were designated by the respective heads of the communities after consultation with the notables and appointed by the government. The council assessed taxes, administered revenues and expenditures, and advised the governor on such questions as he chose to refer to it. As has been said, the system lasted until 1915 when the Ottomans took the opportunity of the war in order to abolish the special autonomous status of Mount Lebanon, and to govern it directly. During the currency of the 1861 constitution, Mount Lebanon was at peace and its inhabitants prospered.

There were many reasons for the success of this system. The Ottoman government as well as the Great Powers, who were its guarantors, had an interest in its continued good functioning. The constitution, again, recognized and made provision for the multiplicity of interests in the province. Also, the manner in which members of the administrative council were chosen conformed to, and made use of, established and familiar methods of informal representation, rather than resorting to formal elections by suffrage alien to local traditions and open to abuse. The constitution was built, as well, on long-standing habits of mutual accommodation between the communities, notably the Maronites and the Druze—habits which, it is true, had been violently disrupted by two decades of mistrust and violence, but which the settlement of 1861 helped to revive. Last, but not least, the rulers of the Mountain had neither the power nor the resources to establish or run an Oriental despotism or the centralized absolutism into which the traditional despotism changed.

It may therefore be said that the autonomous province of Mount Lebanon was the only area of the Middle East in which, for a few decades, there existed a regime recognizably constitutional and representative. After the hiatus of the World War, would the much larger and very different Lebanese Republic be able to carry on in the same tradition? The new political unit had many more Sunnis and Shi'a than the autonomous province. The Sunnis, whether in Beirut or in the Tripoli area, in both of which they predominated, were never happy under the French mandate with being separated from their coreligionists in Syria, and attached to a state where Maronite influence was most powerful, and where the French mandatory was clearly partial to this sect. Indeed, the mandatory had decreed the boundaries of the Lebanese Republic in response to the pleadings and pressures of Maronite notables and ecclesiastical heads who thought it would be good for a Maronite-dominated Lebanon to have the port of Beirut as a capital and outlet to the sea, and similarly to annex as well as Tripoli the areas of Sidon and Tyre in the south, the Bekaa on the east, Rachaya, Hasbaya and Marjayun in the southeast—all areas in which Shi'a generally predominated.

The government of this Greater Lebanon was obviously much more difficult and problematic than that of the autonomous province. The new communities now included in the Republic had entirely different political traditions from the Druze and the Maronites of the Mountain. The Sunnis had formed part of the ruling group of the Ottoman Empire. On the one hand, they had looked upon the imperial government as peculiarly their own, and on the other were accustomed to an administrative set-up in which the subject obeyed the governor, who obeyed the minister, who in turn obeyed the Sultan. They had, between 1918 and 1920 seen, with Faisal's short-lived regime in Damascus, the brilliant prospect of an Arab Sunni state emerging out of the ashes of the Empire. The prospect faded, but the Sunnis of Beirut and Tripoli would still feel much more at home with their fellow-Sunnis in Syria, than in a state where Christians triumphantly basked in the protection of a Power whose feelings of Catholic solidarity were powerful, albeit that in France the state was officially secular. The Sunnis, therefore, would continue to be a discontented and disaffected element in the new Republic.

As for the Shi'a, long accustomed to an inferior position in a Sunni state and traditionally passive in politics, their membership in the new state was not as problematic as the Sunnis'. However, like the Sunnis, and even more than the Sunnis, the mass of the Shi'a would find it difficult, once awakened from their passivity, to participate in unfamiliar political institutions, and to nurture that sense of cohesiveness with the rest of the body politic indispensable to political participation.

Compared with the autonomous province, then, the Lebanese Republic was considerably more heterogeneous. However, the constitution approved by a Lebanese constituent assembly in 1926 showed an essential continuity in outlook with that inherent in the constitution of 1861. A key article in the later constitution lays it down that the various Lebanese communities should be equitably represented in public employments and in the composition of cabinets. Electoral arrangements for the chamber of deputies set up by the constitution showed the same concern for equity in the representation of communities. The country was divided into a number of multi-member constituencies. Voters voted not for a particular candidate, but for one list among many competing for their suffrage. On each list, candidates were drawn from each of the communities inhabiting a particular constituency in a proportion determined by law. Thus, an electoral law of 1950 enacted that in the Beirut constituency there should be elected four Sunnis, one Shi'i, one Maronite, one Greek Catholic, one Greek Orthodox, one Protestant, one Armenian Catholic, two Armenian Gregorians, and one representing all the other, smaller, communities. Voting by list achieved two objectives; it recognized and made provision for the diversity of the electorate, and it obliged candidates from the various communities who had to cohabit in the same list to eschew extreme political positions and to strive for a common ground.

The institutions of the autonomous province had functioned in a satisfactory manner because their work was supervised and guaranteed by the Ottoman suzerain and the European Great Powers who had jointly set it up. Similarly, parliamentary government in the Lebanese Republic pursued an even course so long as there was, so to speak, an authority of last resort which took action, if necessary, to redress the system from the outside if something went wrong with it. This authority was the French High Commissioner with his duties and powers laid down in the mandate. However, after the fall of France, the Allied occupation of the Levant, and the British predominance which followed, the authority of the mandatory was destroyed in Lebanon, as it was in Syria.

The British compelled the Free French to declare the independence of the Lebanese Republic. They also compelled them to ordain elections in the Lebanon as was done in Syria. This British intervention changed the face of Lebanese politics. When the French had been the ultimate authority, rivals in Lebanon could look up only to them and to nobody else. With the British on the scene, and represented moreover by a very belligerent anti-French envoy, Sir Edward Spears, Lebanese politicians and specifically the Maronites among them divided into pro-British and pro-French factions. At the elections of 1943, the pro-British faction won, as was natural, since the British were now considered to be the masters.

The Maronite leader of the winning faction, Bishara al-Khuri, became President of the Republic. Khuri set the Maronites, and the Republic, on a hazardous course. The

Sunnis of Lebanon, as has been said, had been disaffected towards the Republic of which the principal beneficiaries, as they saw it, were the Maronites. Seeing how events were developing, how French power and influence was fast disappearing, and believing that pan-Arabism, patronized by the British, was the wave of the future, Khuri and his Maronite supporters embarked on a new, hitherto untried, policy. They decided to abandon the French connection, seek an understanding with the Sunnis, and attempt to find a lodgment for Lebanon within an Arab world where Arab nationalism was becoming the most powerful current. This policy no doubt tried to come to terms with the underlying weakness of the Maronites in the Republic. Under the French aegis, the Maronites were the dominant group. This dominance was justified on the score of their numerical superiority. Such superiority was however very doubtful. According to the 1932 census, there were 228,000 Maronites in the Republic, as against 178,000 Sunnis and 155,000 Shi'a. This was a much more slender margin than in the autonomous province, where it was estimated in 1868 that Maronites numbered 225,000 and Druze only 25,000. The fact that no census has been taken after 1932 is instructive in this regard, since it was practically certain that such a census would show that Maronites had ceased to be the largest group.

In the face of all this, Khuri's strategy was to seek an understanding with the Sunni leadership. This understanding was encapsulated in what was known as the National Pact. The Pact was not an actual document; it was rather the agreed assumptions on which independent Lebanon would henceforth operate. The terms of this Pact were to the effect that the Maronites would forego any attempt to seek foreign, i.e. French, protection, and that the Sunnis would abandon attempts to seek union with Syria; and that Lebanon would become a member of the "Arab family," while the Arab states would recognize its sovereignty and independence within its existing boundaries.

From a Maronite point of view, the policy made sense in the circumstances, provided that it would hold. In the event, it broke down relatively quickly. In February 1958, a union between Egypt and Syria was effected under Colonel Nasser's leadership. In 1956, the U.S. had procured for him a triumph over the British and the French who had sent a military expedition in order to undo the nationalization of the Suez Canal, and he had become the hero of the Arab world, the Lebanese Sunnis included. A few months after the establishment of the United Arab Republic, a civil war, fomented by the United Arab Republic, and helped by arms and men smuggled from Syria, broke out in Lebanon. There were also internal reasons for the outbreak. It showed however the breakdown of the National Pact, in that the Lebanese Sunnis became very enthusiastic for Nasser and Arab unity under his leadership, and in that an Arab state, far from respecting Lebanese sovereignty and independence, actively interfered in its affairs and sought perhaps also to undo this independence. The episode showed the flimsiness of the National Pact and exhibited a fundamental fault which ran through it. The Pact, in the eyes of those who negotiated it, at any rate certainly in Maronite eyes, served to guard Lebanon against interference in its affairs by Arab states. This proviso, however, in no way bound the Arab states themselves who were not parties to the Pact and could—and would—disregard it at will. In any case, Syria, Lebanon's immediate neighbor, never reconciled itself to the existence of a greater Lebanon, including as it did the Bekaa and Tripoli which in the Syrian view the French had arbitrarily wrenched away and bestowed on their Lebanese protégés. Thus, when Syria and Lebanon became independent, Damascus refused to recognize that Lebanon enjoyed the same sovereignty as other states and accordingly would not exchange ambassadors with Beirut—what need of ambassadors between brethren?

The civil war of 1958 had to be ended by outside intervention, when the U.S. sent troops and naval ships to Beirut out of concern that otherwise Nasserism would sweep through the whole area. Outwardly, the Lebanese government returned to normality, but the tensions which had erupted in the explosion of 1958 remained and, before the 1960s were out, became manifest again in a more acute and ultimately destructive fashion. The 1948 war in Palestine had led large numbers to flee to neighboring countries, including Lebanon. With the passage of the years, the refugee camps in the south, around Beirut and elsewhere became permanent settlements, and in these settlements anti-Israeli guerrilla movements established themselves and gradually became a power in the land. The Lebanese government, and the Maronites in particular, were increasingly alarmed by this considerable threat to the security and authority of the state, and by the danger of Israeli retaliation against attacks mounted from Lebanese territory. The government, however, was prevented from disarming or controlling these guerrilla forces and the settlements in which they found recruits and were able to organize, train and store arms and ammunition. Beirut, the capital of the Republic, was also becoming, in a sense, the capital of the Palestine Liberation Organization.

The Lebanese government was prevented from dealing with this foreign armed force on its territory by the pressure of the Arab states, as well as by Lebanese Sunni opposition. Lebanese governments necessarily included ministers drawn from the main religious groups, and since 1937 the convention had grown, which the National Pact had made into a quasi-law, that while the President of the Republic was a Maronite, the Prime Minister was a Sunni. Without the acquiescence of Sunni ministers, then, it was not possible for the government to order the Lebanese army to control and suppress the PLO fighters and their Lebanese

Sunni followers and sympathizers. This state of affairs simmered, and occasionally exploded in confrontation and disorder from the morrow of the Six-Day War of 1967 to 1975, when a full-scale Lebanese civil war erupted, which blew apart the Lebanese army into its various religious components, paralyzed the administration, and made it impossible for parliamentary government to be carried on. These events fully demonstrated what the incidents of 1958 had already shown—that the National Pact was a hollow construction and that Lebanese society did not have the cohesion necessary to sustain parliamentary government without the kind of support and supervision provided by the Great Powers between 1861 and 1914, and by the French Mandatory between the two world wars.

When the draft of the Lebanese constitution was published in 1926, the Chairman of the drafting commission, justifying article 95 which, it will be recalled, made provision for the equitable representation of the various communities in the organs of the state, declared that the article was necessary because solidarity between communities was not yet so perfect as to make it possible for sectarian interests to be disregarded, and that the Lebanese were not yet accustomed to giving the primacy to patriotic solidarity over sectarian solidarity. Experience since then has shown that sectarian interest and sectarian solidarity have, if anything, become more deeply-rooted in the Lebanese Republic, in a manner such that parliamentary government is not, today, a viable option.

Lebanese military weakness and the inability of Lebanese governments to maintain public order and ward off outside intervention led to a protracted civil war between various militias which exploded in 1975 and is barely at an end. It also led to the armed intervention in Lebanese territory by two neighboring states, Syria and Israel. Beginning in 1976, Syria sent troops into Lebanese territory and occupied the Bekaa and the region of Tripoli. It also established itself in West Beirut, and thus was able actively to intervene in Lebanese politics. Israel invaded Lebanon in June 1982, reaching Beirut early in its campaign. It besieged West Beirut where the PLO leadership and forces had taken refuge. In September, following the Syrian-inspired murder of the Maronite leader Bashir Gemayel, who had just been elected President by majority vote in a rump assembly, to which Bashir's many supporters were brought, it is said, by Israeli good offices and from which Bashir's opponents were absent, Israel briefly occupied West Beirut. Finding the problems and the political and military costs of carrying on the occupation very burdensome, it eventually retreated to a "security zone" in the south.

The Syrians, however, remained in the territories they had occupied in 1976-77, and brought to bear powerful pressure on the Lebanese government, which maintained a ghostly existence, and on various Lebanese factions and their militias. In 1984, the Syrians succeeded in compelling the Lebanese government to disown and denounce a peace treaty which, with the United States' help and mediation, it had signed with Israel the previous year. In 1990, following the invasion of Kuwait, Syria became part of the so-called coalition led by the U.S. against the Iraqi invader. This ensured U.S. complaisance for the complete takeover by Syria of Lebanon, the elimination of all Maronite resistance to its power and influence, and the establishment of a Lebanese government subservient to Syrian wishes. A striking consequence of this Syrian suzerainty may be seen in Lebanese parliamentary government. The last Lebanese elections had taken place in 1972. The disturbed conditions had prevented general elections thereafter, and vacancies in the assembly had mounted in the course of two decades. In 1991, the new Lebanese government, a client of Syria, decided that the 41 vacancies in the assembly should be filled. This was done not through elections, but by the government itself appointing members to the vacant seats. It is a fair assumption that these appointments were vetted and approved beforehand by the Syrian overlord.

The fate of parliamentary government in Lebanon was affected not only by the country's political and military weakness and by the fissiparous character of its polity. It also suffered from the abuse, more or less flagrant, to which it was subjected by leading political figures. Bishara al-Khuri had been elected President of the Republic for a six-year term. According to the constitution the term was not renewable. Khuri, however, desired to serve for another. Parliamentary elections were held, as due, in 1947, two years before the expiry of Khuri's term of office. The elections were rigged, and a pro-Khuri majority eventuated. In 1948 the assembly voted to suspend in Khuri's favor the non-renewal clause, and Khuri was elected for a further term.

This naturally made his competitors and rivals very disgruntled, and their anger increased when parliamentary elections held in 1951 were again rigged by the administration. There was neither a mandatory nor supreme court to appeal to against these irregularities, and Khuri's opponents therefore took their grievances to the streets. Khuri's Maronite rivals, headed by Camille Chamoun—who had been Khuri's supporter over the National Pact policy—acted together with Druze, Sunni and Greek Orthodox figures also opposed to Khuri's regime, in order to organize popular agitation against Khuri's regime, and succeeded in mounting during September 1952 a general strike. The recent *coup d'état* in Egypt which had toppled the king created a heady atmosphere in the Arab world and aroused expectations that reactionary and corrupt regimes could be swept away and replaced by clean and upright rulers. The Lebanese army commander refused to act against the strikers and demonstrators, and Khuri resigned. The assembly, packed with Khuri's supporters, now elected Chamoun to succeed him.

During Chamoun's tenure, two general elections took place, in 1953 and 1957. The President used both occasions to destroy his predecessor's network of clients in the constituencies and to substitute ones of his own. He did this by ingenious gerrymandering. In 1953 he replaced multi-member by single-member constituencies. The object was to destroy the power of the pro-Khuri notables who controlled candidates' lists in multi-member constituencies and who were able to dispense considerable patronage. For the 1957 elections he reestablished multi-member constituencies, having now presumably ensured that candidates' lists would be controlled by notables favorable to him.

During the last year of his tenure, it began to be said that Chamoun wanted, like his predecessor, to be elected for a second term. Chamoun refused to deny these allegations, and at the end of 1957 declared that even though he did not wish the constitution to be amended to allow him to seek a second term, he would have to think again if he felt that the continuity of his policies was in danger. As in 1952, opposition by rivals and opponents became vocal and active. It assumed a more serious and dangerous aspect, as has been said, because of the establishment of the United Arab Republic and the encouragement of civil war from Damascus. The Lebanese Republic was, in the event, saved by U.S. intervention, but at the end of his term Chamoun had to go.

Chamoun was succeeded by the commander of the Lebanese army, Fuad Shihab. He had refused to suppress the demonstrations against Khuri in 1952, and the much more serious disturbances against Chamoun in 1958. His reason was that the discipline and cohesiveness of an army drawn from various communities would be fatally impaired should they be accused of taking sides in internal quarrels. Nor were his fears misplaced, since in the civil war which broke out in 1975 the army burst apart into its various sectarian components. Shihab at any rate was approved of both by the U.S. and Nasser. During his tenure, he took care to be friendly to Nasser and thus gave a new twist to Khuri's National Pact. He also believed that Lebanon was still a collection of communities, and that it had to be transformed into a modern cohesive society through the active intervention of the state. The state, in his view, should promote the welfare of disadvantaged communities, even though this aroused opposition from those that were more affluent. The wealthy in the Lebanese Republic were the Maronites, and the less well off were the Muslims, particularly the Shi'a who were very poor indeed.

Shihab's policies, however, did not increase cohesiveness or solidarity among the communities. What it did was to administer a shock to the traditional society of the south and initiate a process which led the Shi'a to play an increasingly forceful part in Lebanese politics. The effect of Shihab's policies on Shi'i society was compounded by the radical disturbance of the south brought about by Israeli retaliation against PLO guerrillas who, after 1964, and increasingly after 1967, had begun to organize attacks against Israeli civilian targets in northern Galilee. This led to an exodus of Shi'i villagers to Beirut, where they became a volatile mass of squatters, adding a new element to the heterogeneous mixed population of Beirut which, when civil war came, contributed to the ruin of the capital and its division into embattled sectarian zones from which fled all those who did not belong to the particular sect dominating a given zone. The Shi'a were also radicalized and made more belligerent through the inspiration of a new leader, Imam Musa al-Sadr, an Iranian of Lebanese origins who came to the South in the late 1950s and quickly assumed a dominant position in the Shi'i community, supplanting the traditional leadership which was acquiescent of the status quo. He demanded stridently that the state should provide for the welfare of his co-religionists and their defense, caught as they were in the cross-fire between the PLO and Israelis. He organized a mass movement, the Movement of the Deprived, with a military arm, the *Amal*, i.e. Hope, Movement, and launched the idea among his followers that what is not conceded peaceably should be seized by force. Sadr's activity thus contributed to the splintering of Greater Lebanon which the Maronite leaders had so ill-advisedly sought in 1919-20, and the French so unwisely erected. The belated Shi'i explosion in the decade preceding the civil war administered the *coup de grâce* to the prospects of parliamentary government in Lebanon.

V: *Egypt, 1923-1952*

 For the last half century, Egypt has considered itself to be part of the Arab world. This was not always the case. Until Mohammed Ali consolidated his rule, and long afterwards, the majority of the inhabitants of Egypt considered themselves first and foremost as Muslims and subjects of the Ottoman Sultan. Mohammed Ali and his successors endeavored, with some success, to imbue those whom they ruled with the idea that they were first and foremost Egyptians. This was obviously done in the interests of their dynasty.

Following the British occupation in 1882, Egypt, though still nominally part of the Ottoman Empire, became increasingly a separate entity *de facto*. After the war and its sequels, the *de facto* separation became one *de jure*. Until ideas of Arab unity began to be popular in the middle of the Second World War, the intellectual and official class held that Egypt had a distinct personality of its own which could be traced down the centuries from Pharaonic times onwards.

As has been said, however, public discourse in Egypt now assumes without question that it is an Arab country. This justifies taking its political experience into account in any description of Arab political culture.

Before and after the British occupation, Egypt remained an autocracy. Nothing, in theory, limited the autocracy of the Khedives (as Mohammed Ali's successors came to be known), except the Sultan's own shadowy autocracy. After 1882, the advice of the British Agent and Consul-General in Cairo was advice which had to be followed. In practice, he, therefore, possessed ultimate authority which only his own government in London could control and modify.

It is true that in 1883, there were established a legislative council and a legislative assembly, small bodies, most of the members of which were appointed, and who could exercise no effective control over public affairs. In 1913, these two bodies were merged into a new-style legislative assembly in which 17 members were government appointees and 66 elected by indirect suffrage. The assembly was in no sense legislative, but rather predominantly consultative. The new assembly met in 1914, but the outbreak of war shortly afterwards ended its meetings.

The end of the war brought great and unexpected changes in Egyptian politics. When the Ottomans joined the war against the Allies, the British declared Egypt a British protectorate, and at the Paris Peace Conference in 1919 obtained international recognition of the new status. At this point, they contemplated no change in the governance of Egypt, as it had been carried on after 1882.

Unlike Iraq, Syria or Lebanon, Egypt was not a mandated territory where the League of Nations laid responsibilities on the mandatory to promote self-governing representative institutions, but by a curious concatenation of circumstances, the British found themselves in 1922 pressing the then-ruler of Egypt to do just this.

This ruler was Fuad, a brother of the Khedive Tawfiq, who had never expected to ascend to such a position. His nephew, the Khedive Abbas II, had been on bad terms with the British who considered him an intriguer and a thorn in their flesh. When war broke out, he was on a visit to Istanbul. He was told not to come back and was deposed. An uncle was proclaimed Sultan in his place, his change of title marking the end of subordination to the Ottoman Sultan. When he died in 1917, the British thought that Fuad would be a safe replacement. They proved mistaken.

Fuad turned out to be both very ambitious and a greater master of intrigue than his nephew. Fuad was determined to secure his own position, of which he could not be absolutely sure so long as his nephew was alive (Fuad, in fact, predeceased Abbas) and thus conceivably able to seek to regain the rulership of Egypt. Fuad also saw no reason why he should remain subservient to the British, or why he should not exercise to the full the autocracy which his ancestors from Mohammed Ali to Ismail had exercised.

President Wilson's Fourteen Points, with their emphasis on self-determination, gave Fuad an opening to challenge the British Protectorate when the war ended. Together with some Egyptian political figures, he concerted an approach to the British High Commissioner— as the British representative came to be called when the Protectorate was proclaimed.

The approach was to request that an Egyptian delegation should proceed to London and discuss with British ministers the future government of Egypt, which the proclamation of the Protectorate had left undefined. Those making the request, two days after the Armistice with Germany, were three political figures, who then were holding no office, and of whom the best known was Saad Zaghlul.

Zaghlul, then in his sixties, had had by then a long political career. He had been appointed Minister of Education in 1906 and of Justice in 1910. He was then considered to be pro-British, and he was on bad terms with Khedive Abbas. In fact, he resigned his office in 1912, after a clash with the Khedive.

Shortly afterwards, however, he became the Khedive's supporter and defended his interests in the Legislative Assembly, to which he was elected and where he served as vice president. This stance displeased the British authorities and cast him under a cloud. When the session of the assembly was terminated, he retired into private life, and until Fuad's accession, Zaghlul made no secret of his continuing loyalty to Abbas, whom he considered to be the rightful ruler.

Soon after Fuad became Sultan, Zaghlul seems to have transferred his loyalty to the new ruler and became an adviser and confidant. Fuad proposed him for ministerial office, but the British, wary of his record since 1914, vetoed the proposal.

The approach to the High Commissioner in November 1918 met with a swift refusal from ministers in London. They were preoccupied with the forthcoming peace conference, and the long years of British control over Egypt, with hardly a challenge, made them complacent and contemptuous.

This rebuff created a political crisis in Egypt. The Egyptian ministers, who had served all through the war, now resigned. Because they had cooperated with the British and helped in satisfying the demands of British commanders who were in Egypt to carry on the war against the Ottomans, they were afraid that if they did not protest against this rebuff by resigning, they could be upstaged by both Fuad and Zaghlul, who would thus be able to further their own aims at the ministers' expense.

Zaghlul, again, started organizing country-wide petitions in favor of his delegation, or Wafd, proceeding to Europe to discuss the future of Egypt. The circulation of these petitions must have entailed a great deal of organization and could not have been done without the cooperation of the Egyptian administration and of the royal palace, which wielded a great deal of influence.

When the ministers resigned in March 1919, Zaghlul made a move which took Fuad by surprise. He went to the palace as the head of a delegation and left a menacing letter, warning the Sultan that he should not seek to appoint new ministers against the "will of the people" and referring to the "temporary and illegal protectorate" which had conferred the sultanate on him. Zaghlul was clearly setting out to be the people's tribune—which nothing in his previous career would have led Fuad or anyone else in political circles to expect. In response, Fuad, who had set this particular ball rolling, asked for the protection of the Protectorate. The Protectorate obliged and deported Zaghlul and some companions to Malta.

The deportation was followed by widespread country-wide disorders. In fact, the war had made the country volatile. There had been inflation which bore heavily on the poor, and a relaxation of British control over the Egyptian administration which left the door open for an increase in corruption by local officials and notables. There had also been the requisition of laborers and animals needed in the war against the Ottomans, which was left to the same local officials and notables to administer and which increased their opportunities to act arbitrarily and oppressively.

For all this, the British, whom the population had learned over the decades to consider as the ultimate authority, were naturally blamed. The volatility was appreciably increased by the circulation of petitions in favor of Zaghlul's delegation, a proceeding hitherto unheard of, and which people took to indicate that the British were becoming weaker and losing their grip.

The British Prime Minister and his Foreign Secretary decided to appoint Lord Allenby, who had successfully led the final campaign against the Ottomans in the Levant, as Special High Commissioner, for the purpose of reestablishing law and order and asserting British authority. By the time Allenby arrived in Egypt towards the end of March 1919, the disturbances had been quelled to all intents and purposes by the British forces in Egypt. Allenby, however, decided that a spectacular political initiative was needed to show that conciliation was being combined with firmness. He therefore had Zaghlul and his companions released from Malta. They went to Paris where the Peace Conference was in session, and where they sought in vain to prevent recognition of the British protectorate over Egypt.

Allenby's action was interpreted as an indication of British weakness and a proof of Zaghlul's strength. Zaghlul now could claim that he was the sole representative and spokesman of the Egyptian people, that the people had revolted in support of his actions, and that the British had willy-nilly to deal with him alone.

The British government, which had appointed Allenby and seen him take action quite the opposite of what it had intended, took another step in response to the uprising which also had quite unexpected consequences. It appointed a member of the Cabinet, Lord Milner, to head a commission to investigate Egyptian grievances and suggest remedies. Milner had served some two decades before as a high official in the Egyptian government and was supposed to know the country well. He also believed that Allenby had made a great mistake in releasing Zaghlul. His commission did not come to Egypt until the end of 1919.

By then Zaghlul had had time to mobilize his supporters and establish relations with a secret terrorist apparatus which had been in existence since the first decade of the century. A boycott of the commission was enforced by intimidation. Political figures refused out of fear to meet the commission and declared that Zaghlul was the only leader who could speak on behalf of Egypt.

Milner and his fellow commissioners stayed in Egypt until March 1920. Faced by the boycott, the clamor and the abuse which accompanied their stay, Milner and his fellow commissioners persuaded themselves that it would be best for Britain to divest itself of all responsibility for the good government of Egypt, and simply to ensure vital British interests by means of a treaty with Egypt which would have to be ratified by a representative assembly.

In the General Conclusions, which they set down at the end of their stay, the commissioners recognized the limitations of such an assembly. They declared that "owing to the backwardness of the mass of the people, of whom ninety percent are quite illiterate, it will be many years before any elected Assembly is really representative of more than a comparatively limited class." They saw that parliamentary government under the social conditions then obtaining meant oligarchical government "and, if wholly uncontrolled, it would be likely to show little regard for the interests of the Egyptian people." A few months later, an Egyptian former minister, visiting London, went to see a member of the Milner commission. What he had to say confirmed, from a different perspective, the judgment of the commission. Parliamentary government, he declared, would hand Egypt over to a dominant class "who would manipulate elections and purchase votes—the whole system of administration by *baksheesh* [i.e. bribery] would start afresh and the fellah would undoubtedly be oppressed."

After returning to London, Milner was persuaded by a personal adviser and by a former Egyptian minister, Adli Pasha, that it would be a good idea for him to invite Zaghlul, who was still in Paris, to come to London for personal talks in the hope that he could be persuaded to facilitate negotiation of the treaty which Milner and his fellow commissioners had in mind. Without obtaining the cabinet's permission, or even consulting them, Milner invited Zaghlul, in his personal capacity, to visit London for private discussions. Zaghlul hastened to advertise the invitation, describing it as an official invitation from the British Colonial Secretary to himself as Leader of the Egyptian Wafd. This enhanced Zaghlul's stature in Egypt enormously, to the consternation and dismay of Fuad and of Zaghlul's political rivals.

Milner's negotiations with Zaghlul were long-drawn out, and ostensibly ended with an agreement in which Milner, still acting on his own, without any authority, conceded a great deal of what Zaghlul demanded. Zaghlul promised to recommend the agreement to the Egyptian people. He did nothing of the kind, but put it about that he could have obtained much more if Adli, who had accompanied him to London, had not queered his pitch.

All of Milner's concessions were meant to ensure that an Anglo-Egyptian treaty, reserving essential British interests, would be signed. It proved impossible for this to be done. Zaghlul, now back from exile, but with no official responsibilities to impose restraint on his words, was claiming that he was the sole representative of the people, who would work to secure full independence for them. No political figure dared to demand anything less than Zaghlul was demanding. Matters reached a deadlock. Allenby sought to break the deadlock by reaching agreement with some of Zaghlul's rivals, banishing Zaghlul outside Egypt, and forcing his own government against its will and better judgment to abrogate the Protectorate without prior signature of a treaty, the sole object of Milner's maladroit and unsuccessful strategy.

Allenby was able, forcefully, to execute this *coup d'état*, the elements of which are encapsulated in his Declaration of February 28, 1922. This Declaration recognized Egyptian independence subject to reservations unilaterally laid down by the British, but in which no Egyptian government was ever to acquiesce. In preparing his *coup d'état*, Allenby made a deal with some of Zaghlul's rivals. They would take office and stand up to the Zaghlulists in defense of the Declaration. In return, Allenby would see to it that Egypt was endowed with a constitution and a parliament. In fact, the draft of the Declaration contained a sentence to the effect that the British government would "view with favor the creation of a Parliament with right to control the policy and administration of a constitutional, responsible government." It was then, through the fiat of the autocratic and blundering Allenby, in the wake of Milner's blunders, which had themselves followed on Allenby's initial blunders, that Egypt came to be endowed with a constitutional government.

The politicians with whom Allenby had reached an understanding belonged to a tradition which dated from the first decade of the twentieth century. It had been nurtured by a few cultivated Egyptians who admired Western political thought and institutions, and with whom Zaghlul himself had then been associated. Shortly after they took office, following Allenby's Declaration, they formed a party to counter Zaghlul's Wafd, the name of which indicates their political preferences. They called it the Liberal Constitutionalist Party. It was, therefore, somewhat ironic that the constitution to which they aspired, they should have obtained through an autocrat's intervention.

Constitutions and parliaments were not to the taste of the other autocrat in Egypt, King Fuad (the new and grander title which he substituted for Sultan following the Declaration). He, however, could not resist Allenby's pressure since, Declaration or no Declaration, there was still an Army of Occupation in Egypt which would do the High Commissioner's bidding. A commission was appointed in April 1922 to draft a constitution in which the Liberal Constitutionalists were liberally represented. After six months, it produced a draft constitution which began by declaring that all authority derived from the nation. It provided for a two-chamber parliament exercising legislative power, while the executive would be a council of ministers holding office so long as it retained the legislature's confidence. The King, however, had the power to appoint and dismiss ministers and dissolve parliaments. He also had a limited power to veto legislation.

Fuad did not like the draft, which clearly limited his hitherto unlimited powers. He disliked the ministers who had made the deal with Allenby, and suspected, rightly, that such a constitution meant not that the nation would exercise ultimate authority, but that his own power would simply pass into the hands of ministers. His suspicion was akin to Abd al-Hamid's suspicion of Midhat's constitution.

Fuad took up again the old liaison with Zaghlul, letting it be known that he favored the Patriot's return from exile, which was being prevented by the ministers' opposition. The Wafd had attacked the constitutional commission, and was now emboldened to attack the administration as one imposed by the British, which was, in fact, true. The position of the ministers was thus undermined, and they resigned in December 1922. Their successors were King's men who worked to amend the draft constitution and increase considerably Fuad's powers.

The amended draft gave him sole control of religious endowments and institutions, with all the great financial and political power which this conferred. The presidency of the senate was given to the King to confer at his discretion and the number of the senators appointed by him appreciably increased. He also had the power to appoint and dismiss military officers and diplomats. It was this amended draft which was promulgated by royal decree, a gift, so to speak, from the sovereign to the people, in April 1923.

In accordance with the constitution, elections were called for December 1923. Prior to this, Zaghlul returned, in September, and there was clear evidence that the Wafd and the royal court were acting hand-in-hand. Wafdist newspapers received large subsidies from the Palace, and Wafdist intimidation and terrorism showed a recrudescence. The elections naturally produced a Wafdist landslide, and Zaghlul became Prime Minister.

Two features of Zaghlul's administration, which lasted for about a year, are worth noticing. In the first place, though Zaghlul had an overwhelming majority, an appreciable number of his ministers were not Wafdists but King's men. This would confirm that a bargain between him and the King had been struck before the elections, and that in exchange for his support, Fuad would have his representatives in the council of ministers. In the second place, however, the wily Zaghlul could not willingly agree to have his power limited by Fuad. As he had done in 1919, he now also tried to overawe Fuad. To do so, his men organized tumultuous demonstrations against the King. It is impossible to say how the clash would have ended if Zaghlul had stayed long in power.

His tenure unexpectedly came to an end at the end of 1924 when the British Governor-General of the Sudan, who was *ex officio* head of the Egyptian Army, was murdered by members of Zaghlul's terrorist apparatus, whose head had been tried and imprisoned by the British in 1920, but whom Zaghlul pardoned and released when he assumed office. The assassination, which showed that Zaghlul had an imperfect control over this apparatus, outraged Allenby. In retaliation he imposed, without authority from British ministers, harsh measures on Egypt. This gave Fuad justification to dismiss Zaghlul, in spite of his parliamentary majority, and to dissolve the chamber of deputies.

As may be seen, the beginnings of constitutional and parliamentary government in Egypt were the unexpected outcome of much intrigue on the part of Fuad, Zaghlul and other Egyptian figures, and of many egregious blunders by British officials in Egypt, by British ministers, by Allenby and by Milner and his fellow commissioners. It is a complicated and bizarre overture to some thirty years of failed attempts to govern Egypt through representative institutions, a failure which culminated in the military *coup d'état* of July 1952, the deposition of Faruq, Fuad's son and successor, and the abolition of the monarchy.

The failure of parliamentary government in Egypt was implicit in its beginnings. The granting of a constitution and the establishment of a parliament were imposed by a foreign power, whose representative had become involved in an intrigue with some local politicians. The King, with all the traditional influence which the royal court had in the country, and with the restraints on his power by the British gradually diminishing after the Declaration of

February 28, 1922, was opposed to a constitution and a parliament which would limit his autocracy. Zaghlul who, after 1919, had so unexpectedly become the most prominent figure in Egyptian politics, sought to exercise undivided power by intimidating both the King and his fellow politicians. The instrument he used for this purpose was the Wafd which he claimed to be not a political party in any ordinary sense but the spokesman of the Egyptian nation.

In the four years between his sudden emergence in 1919, and his electoral triumph at the end of 1923, Zaghlul had discovered in himself remarkable demagogic powers with which he could move the mass and inspire in them a fervid, if inchoate, enthusiasm. He was right in rejecting the appellation "party" for the Wafd. It was indeed a new Middle Eastern phenomenon, what might more properly be called a movement, used to mobilize the multitude in order to attain power, rather than an organization representing a particular interest or class, and designed for parliamentary give-and-take or thrust-and-parry. To illustrate Zaghlul's power to arouse and mobilize, I still recall the words of an elderly Egyptian professor whom I met about 1960, who was then still powerfully impressed with Zaghlul's leadership. To show the breadth and the depth of this appeal, he declared that it was the fellah's belief that even the mooing cows in the field were calling, Zaghlul, Zaghlul! It was by no means certain that the professor himself did not, in some part of his mind, believe that Zaghlul's appeal extended even to the cows.

In contrast to this movement, with its total dependence on the power of a single leader to inspire and arouse, the other political groups which played a part on the scene of Egyptian parliamentary politics may accurately be described as factions, factions made up of Cairo politicians who, by virtue of their connections with the Palace or with the British, and by their Western-style education, were able to operate in the political corridors of the capital, forever making ephemeral combinations and momentary alliances dictated by the prospect of immediate profit, and as quickly unmade when changing circumstances so required. The Liberal Constitutionalists, with whom Allenby made a deal in 1922 and against whom the King and Zaghlul combined in 1923, are very much a case in point, the more so that unlike other, later factions, they prided themselves on acting according to a set of political principles of which their name was the emblem.

When the King dismissed Zaghlul and dissolved parliament at the end of 1924, he formed a government composed mainly of his own followers, but the Liberal Constitutionalists did not find it against their principles to share office with colleagues who were nothing more than servants of the royal court. For a year or so, the King reigned supreme over Egyptian politics. However, a British High Commissioner who succeeded Allenby, Lord Lloyd, found that the King's rule meant despotism and corruption. He indicated to Fuad that new elections should be held, and the King had to give way. The elections duly registered his defeat in the Cairo political game, and a Wafdist majority was returned. Lloyd, however, vetoed the return of Zaghlul to office, and the Liberal Constitutionalist, Adli, formed a coalition government composed of Wafdists and of the same Liberal Constitutionalists who had previously taken part in a coalition with the King's men.

Zaghlul died in 1927, and with his death, Lloyd's veto against a Wafdist government disappeared. Zaghlul's successor, Mustafa al-Nahhas, claimed the right of the majority to form a government and became prime minister. Fuad's antipathy to the Wafd was unabated. He accused Nahhas of corruption and misuse of influence and dismissed him. To succeed Nahhas, he appointed Mohammed Mahmud, the leader of the Liberal Constitutionalists. Mohammed Mahmud had cheerfully taken part in the anti-Wafdist coalition of 1925, as well as in the Wafdist-led coalition of 1926. Now he, leading a party which stood for constitutional and parliamentary government, as cheerfully dissolved the parliament, postponed elections for three years and governed by decree.

Fuad died in 1936, when his son Faruq was a minor. He assumed full powers only the following year. He found in office a Wafdist government led by Nahhas and enjoying an overwhelming parliamentary majority. He dismissed Nahhas and appointed Mohammed Mahmud prime minister. Again, Mohammed Mahmud dissolved the parliament. This time, however, he did call new elections. They duly took place, and naturally produced an overwhelming anti-Wafdist majority.

The behavior of other political parties, so-called, was just as blatantly factional as that of the Liberal Constitutionalists. There was the Unionist Party, formed of King's men after Zaghlul's downfall in 1924. There was the People's Party which existed between 1930 and 1933 when Ismail Sidqi was prime minister, appointed by Fuad to succeed yet another Wafdist government which he had had to appoint in response to British pressure and which he was able to dismiss in 1930. The People's Party consisted simply of Sidqi's followers and disappeared when he fell from power. There was, again, the Saadist Party formed by some Wafdist figures who fell out with Nahhas in 1937, who claimed to be Zaghlul's true heirs, in token of which they adopted his first name as the name of the Party. There was also the Kutla, i.e., the Bloc, formed by another ex-Wafdist, William Makram Obeid, who had been Nahhas' right-hand man, but who quarreled bitterly with him and left the Wafd in 1942. Shortly after this falling out, Obeid, inspired and abetted by Faruq, wrote and circulated a Black Book in which he revealed the financial corruption and the peculations of the Wafd which he had been able closely to observe as the Wafdist minister of finance.

By the time the Black Book appeared, the Wafd had been transformed from a movement into yet another political faction. Nahhas was devoid of his predecessor's charisma and demagogic abilities. For a long time, however, Nahhas and the Wafd were able to live off Zaghlul's legacy. Interestingly enough, the effects of this legacy were most apparent not in Egyptian politics, but in Anglo-Egyptian relations. Milner, it will be recalled, engaged in negotiations with Zaghlul in 1920, even though Zaghlul then held no official position. He did so in the belief that Zaghlul, in some sense, represented the Egyptian people, and that if he came to agree on a treaty with him, when this fell to be ratified by an Egyptian assembly, the assembly would consist overwhelmingly of Zaghlul's supporters. As has been seen, it did not prove possible then to conclude such a treaty. Zaghlul proved a slippery customer, and, subsequently, no other Egyptian political figure dared demand anything less than Zaghlul for fear of being upstaged.

A treaty defining Anglo-Egyptian relations remained the aspiration of successive British governments. In 1929, the Labor government in London, strong in the belief that a party like itself, speaking for the people, would have little difficulty in reaching agreement with another party which also spoke for the people, determined that a Wafd government would be the best negotiating partner. Mohammed Mahmud resigned. Nahhas succeeded him in January 1930, and elections naturally returned a Wafdist majority. The negotiations failed, principally because Nahhas insisted that the Sudan, which had been conquered by Mohammed Ali, should come under the Egyptian crown. This demand had been formulated by Zaghlul, and his successor could demand no less, as neither could any other politician for fear of being outbid by his rivals. Nahhas, too, may have thought that an "anti-imperialist" party, such as Labor, would concede the demand, the more so since they were eager to conclude a treaty. Zaghlul had made the same mistake in 1924 when he was prime minister and a Labor government was in office. He travelled to London in high hopes and came back to Cairo trailing failure. Neither in 1924 or in 1930 would the Labor government, for all its anti-imperialism, give up the Sudan.

When Nahhas and the British found it impossible to agree on a treaty, Fuad dismissed the Wafd government. The parliament was dissolved, and the new prime minister, Ismail Sidqi, introduced a new constitution giving greater powers to the King, and substituting indirect for direct elections. The new parliament had, as usual, a majority which supported the existing administration.

During 1935-6, a conservative government in London again sought to conclude a treaty with Egypt. It, too, believed that only the Wafd could deliver the consent of the Egyptian people. The 1923 constitution was reinstated and elections called under the original dispensation. On this occasion, in a novel and original arrangement, the Wafd and the other parties divided up beforehand their share of seats in the forthcoming elections. The elections naturally resulted in a Wafdist majority. Nahhas formed a government and this time an Anglo-Egyptian treaty was at last signed, with the Sudan issue left in abeyance. As has been said, Faruq assumed full royal powers in 1937. His antipathy to the Wafd was as great as his father's. He quickly dismissed Nahhas and the Wafdist parliament was dissolved.

The Wafd remained in the wilderness until February 1942, various factions in various combinations succeeding one another in office. By then, the Second World War was raging, and the British were seriously threatened in the vital Mediterranean and Middle Eastern theater by the Afrika Korps. The security situation within Egypt itself was becoming parlous, and it was feared that rampant pro-Axis sympathies were being encouraged by the King who, in fact, was in communication with both Italy and Germany.

Twenty years, almost to the day, after Allenby's February 1922 Declaration, another *coup d'état* was carried out by the British representative, now called an ambassador. In February 1942, Sir Miles Lampson surrounded the royal palace with tanks and armed troops, and then marched into Faruq's presence, flanked by a general with a revolver in his holster, and delivered an ultimatum. Either Nahhas would be asked by the King to form a government, or the King would be deposed.

These events showed the bankruptcy both of Allenby's Declaration of 1922 and of the 1936 treaty, both of which rested on the premise that Egypt's internal affairs should be left to the Egyptians, and that only in this way would British interests in Egypt be preserved. The record shows that to preserve their interests, the British had to intervene repeatedly in Egyptian politics. In fact, until the end of the Second World War, Egyptian politics can be described as a minuet with three dancers: the King, the British and the Cairo politicians. The Egyptian people could not even be described as spectators at the show, since the wheelings and the pirouettes took place on a stage largely hidden from them. Their only function was to cast the votes which the pretense of elections occasionally required. Even this function was often dispensed with, as is described in a famous autobiographical novel by Tawfiq al-Hakim, titled *The Maze of Justice* in its English translation, where one of the duties of the officials during elections in the countryside was the stuffing of ballot-boxes.

The *coup d'état* of February 1942 also destroyed the long-lived illusion that the Wafd was the genuine representative of the Egyptian people. The illusion was created by the cumulative blunders of Fuad, Allenby and Milner during 1919-20, and by Zaghlul's consummate ability to extract from them the utmost advantage in building for himself a reputation as the people's tribune. Following the disastrous end of his administration at the end of 1924, Zaghlul was a spent force, but his legend was potent enough to cover the Wafd with a magical sheen which, however, took in chiefly the British government, until they themselves rudely shattered the illusion in 1942. In effect, for all its populism, the Wafd, from a movement, had quickly become one faction among the others in the political marketplace, engaging in the same intrigues and generously helping itself, when occasion offered, to the sweets of office, licit, and, more usually, forbidden.

In 1944, the dangers of war having receded from the Middle East, the British no longer had an interest in maintaining the Wafd in office. Faruq was able to dismiss Nahhas, and Egypt was, until the summer of 1949, governed by the usual factional combinations. During these years, however, Egypt became increasingly volatile and more difficult to govern. The economy was stagnant and quite unable to provide employment for the relentlessly increasing population. The Palestine War of 1948, which Egypt entered at the last minute at Faruq's behest, ended disastrously. All these developments meant that there was a steady rise in public disorder, which was exacerbated by various movements which had come on the scene during the 1930s, but had been more or less suppressed by the British, with the help of the Wafd, during the war years. These movements, whether Islamic, leftist or nationalist, sought to mobilize the mass, of which schoolboys and university students now formed a particularly crucial element, in order to use it as a weapon against the regime, very much as Zaghlul had done in his heyday. By the summer of 1949, Faruq seems to have decided that the situation required that he should recruit the Wafd to his side. A coalition government was formed in which the Wafd took part. This government organized elections which took place in January 1950 which naturally gave the victory to the Wafd, and Nahhas thereupon presided over his fourth, and last, administration.

Ever since the Declaration of February 1922, the dialectic of inter-factional dispute and rivalry had been driven by the ever-present issue of Anglo-Egyptian relations. After, as before the 1936 treaty, the British were in control of the Sudan, and they kept troops in Egypt. These issues were stilled for a time during the war, but they revived after 1945. Successive administrations put the revision of the treaty at the top of their agenda and sought to persuade or force the British to satisfy their desiderata. They failed. Nahhas too, took up the issue, and negotiated with the British between March 1950 and October 1951. He also failed. The government then decided, or felt compelled, to try conclusions with the British. It unleashed or encouraged guerrilla attacks against British forces in their Suez base. The British reacted forcibly. On January 25, 1952, they ordered the Egyptian police and gendarmerie in Ismailiyya to vacate the town in order to ensure that it could not be used to mount attacks on British installations. On orders of the Minister of the Interior, the police and gendarmerie refused to go, and the British destroyed the police barracks, killing over 50 policemen. The next day, riots started in Cairo, large parts of the center of which were set on fire.

On January 27, Faruq dismissed Nahhas. The military *coup d'état* of July 23 deposed and exiled the King, put an end to the rule of Mohammed Ali's dynasty, abolished the 1923 constitution and its parliamentary institutions, and disbanded all political parties, the Wafd included. Since that time, Zaghlul's creation, which had occasioned such awe as a mighty and irresistible force, fell into the silence of oblivion.

VI: The Failure of Constitutionalism and its Aftermath

The story of constitutional and representative government in the leading countries of the Arab world, as examined above, may be supplemented by essentially similar stories in two other Arab countries, the geographical position and political importance of which place them on the fringes of the Arab world. These are Libya and the Sudan.

Libya became a parliamentary monarchy in 1951. It was poor, sparsely populated, its extensive territory mostly desert, and its only important center the city of Tripoli, which is the capital. As elsewhere in the Arab world, more so even, votes, elections, and parliamentary institutions were highly unfamiliar. Libya might have gone on vegetating in its impoverished state had it not been that oil was discovered and exploited by foreign oil companies, which brought, to start with, a modest amount of riches, but which raised expectations, thus complicating the governance of the kingdom. The government also complicated matters for itself by promoting education, and particularly military education. It was hoped that this would supply a corps of technically proficient and qualified officers for the Army, which the government believed necessary to maintain. As happened elsewhere in the Middle East, the exposure of young officers to modern military education meant at the same time exposure to radical ideas. In the case of Libya, the ideas in question were those which went under the label of Nasserism. These ideas were pertinaciously promoted by the Egyptian government through the press and, above all, through radio broadcasts. After the Suez affair of 1956, Nasserism began to have an increasingly wide audience in the Arab world, particularly among the young. It denounced corruption and reaction which it claimed to be responsible for the weakness and division of the Arab world. Nasserism was the sovereign remedy which would bring about unity, prosperity and a just society.

Some Libyan officers proved to be some of Colonel Nasser's most fervent admirers. In September 1969, they carried out a *coup d'état* which toppled the monarchy and the constitution. Their leader was Colonel Mu'ammar al-Qadhafi who looked upon himself as the heir of Colonel Nasser, destined to realize his mentor's vision, a mentor whose reputation had been fatally undermined by the debacle of 1967 but who still attracted great devotion as a lost leader whose message still retained its truth and attractive power.

Since Qadhafi's *coup d'état*, Libya has been ruled by him and his fellow officers. Like Nasser and his *Philosophy of the Revolution*, he has produced, in *The Third Theory*, an ideology which purports to explain the past and present and to plan the future.

He has also established a new kind of regime, for which he has coined a new term, *jamahiriyya*. The term is intended to distinguish this regime from an ordinary kind of republic, which in Arabic is called *jumhuriyya*. *Jumhuriyya* derives from *jumhur*, classically meaning the populace, and currently, the public. *Jumhuriyya* is thus the exact counterpart of *respublica*. *Jamahiriyya* derives from *jamahir*, the plural of *jumhur*. It may be translated as the masses, and *jamahiriyya* may be understood to mean a people's republic as, with a similar pleonasm, the states of the Soviet empire used to call themselves peoples' democracies.

The Libyan *jamahiriyya*, as designed by Qadhafi, foreswears all representation and representative assemblies because they distort the peoples' will. The regime instead professes to promote the government of the people directly by the people. Since, however, Libya is territorially extensive, since it has to have a relatively complex administrative structure, and since the last word rests, in practice, with he who controls the armed forces, to govern Libya by means of a series of town meetings must partake either of fantasy or make-believe. The reality is, as elsewhere, military rule.

The other state on the periphery of the Arab world was the Sudan, which from 1898 had been administered formally as an Anglo-Egyptian condominium, but in reality by the British governor-general and British officials who ran the administration both in the capital, Khartoum, and in the provinces. As has been seen, the Egyptian government claimed that the Sudan should come under the Egyptian crown. They persisted in this claim. In 1923, Fuad tried to insert a clause to this effect in the Egyptian constitution, abandoning the attempt only in response to Allenby's threats. Following the breakdown of Anglo-Egyptian negotiation in October 1950, Faruq was unilaterally proclaimed King of Egypt and the Sudan. The military regime which succeeded the monarchy, however, gave up this claim in order to obtain complete British evacuation of Egypt in the Anglo-Egyptian treaty of 1954.

The Sudan became a republic in 1956. In 1948, the British had set up a legislative assembly, and in 1953, following Anglo-Egyptian agreement, general elections for a parliament were held. The elections were contested principally by two parties, one in favor of independence, and the other of the Egyptian connection. The latter won and formed a government. Its leaders eventually changed their minds and opted for independence. Parliamentary government, after independence, lasted for just under three years. It proved difficult and ultimately unworkable. The rifts which existed in the country were too deep and irreconcilable to allow constitutional parliamentary government to function.

The less serious rift, serious enough however, was that between the two main parties which reflected longstanding and deeply-held sectarian differences in the Muslim north between the followers of the Sudanese Mahdi (who had set up the Mahdist state in 1881 and which the British destroyed in 1898) and his opponents. The more serious rift, which has become increasingly unbridgeable, was that between the Muslim majority in the north and the Christian and pagan south.

In November 1958, the commander-in-chief of the Sudanese Army carried out a *coup d'état* and instituted a military regime. It lasted for six years. In October 1964, public tumults led to indiscriminate shooting of a crowd by machine-gun fire. Young Army officers objected to this and insisted on returning to their barracks. The commander-in-chief, who had also become prime minister and minister of defense, shortly afterwards found himself compelled to retire. Civilian governments succeeded the military regime. They lasted for a period under five years, confronting perpetual dissensions and increasing fear by the southerners of what the Muslims of the north held in store for them.

In May 1969, Colonel Ja'far al-Numayri carried out another *coup d'état*. He ruled until 1985 when a fellow officer executed a *coup d'état* against him and took the succession. His regime lasted for about a year, and was followed by a number of civilian governments, having to face a civil war in the south and sectarian turmoil in the north, until another officer intervened with yet another *coup d'état* in 1989.

The record, then, of constitutional and representative government in the Arab world is thus disappointing, not to say dismal. The manner in which it was introduced, by foreign fiat or direction, and the peculiar conditions in which it had to function in each country meant that it could not be government by discussion and compromise, in which the supremacy of the law was unchallenged. Rather, it meant government in which the reality was ballot-rigging, gerrymandering, administrative arbitrariness, and large-scale corruption, and where elections and parliaments were, and were known to be, a make-believe and a deception. To use the term which figures in the title of a widely-read book, the age in which these events happened was not a liberal age. It was, rather, a disreputable age in which the official and intellectual classes increasingly felt distaste and contempt for anything which might be described as liberal.

The failure everywhere of constitutional and representative government was due not only to its incompatibility with local political traditions, but also to the shape given to the political institutions of these states under the influence of their foreign sponsors. Leaving Lebanon aside, everywhere else it was the so-called Westminster model which was adopted. These governments were supposed to be responsible to an elected assembly which is the depository of the legal sovereignty of the state. This arrangement was indeed a workable one at Westminster because, to use the distinction made by the well-known British constitutional lawyer, A.V. Dicey, the legal sovereignty exercised by the Queen-in-Parliament (in British constitutional parlance) had, at the back of it, political sovereignty inherent in the people. The significance of this political sovereignty was that the people could, through elections, change the complexion of a legislative assembly and hence the complexion of a government. But if it was the government which controlled and dictated the outcome of elections, then the Westminster model, from being the guarantor of legality and public freedoms, turns into an instrument of unrestrained despotism, as it has proved to be both in the Arab world and in Africa.

On the other hand, what might be called the Washington model, with its separation of the legislative, executive and judiciary, each exercising original powers which the two other branches of government cannot trench upon, provides a specific against the arbitrariness inherent in the perversion of the Westminster model. The Washington model has never been tried in the Arab world, and it may well be that, had it been tried, it would also have been, for one reason or another, denatured out of all recognition.

The disfavor into which parliamentary government fell in the Arab world from the 1930s onwards was due not only to its manifest corruption, but also to the spread of other political ideas which seemed to promise greater success. In their heyday, Fascism, and particularly Nazism, seemed to offer a strong challenge to constitutional government, to be indeed the wave of the future. These ideologies seemed to promise efficiency, strength and prosperity. They seemed also to create political cohesion and to enhance the attachment of the population to the leader and increase their readiness to sacrifice themselves for the cause articulated and promoted by him. This, of course, was no small thing for rulers who governed deeply-fractured polities where the governed felt little loyalty for governments set over them through some foreign manipulation or circumstances over which they had no control. The widespread enthusiasm which Fascism and Nazism evoked within the intellectual and official class, replacing the earlier belief in representative government, was disappointed by the defeat of the Axis Powers which had seemed at the outset to sweep all before them.

After 1945, Socialist ideology, with its promise of prosperity and equality through centralized economic planning, attracted similar enthusiasm. If the Young Turk officers and their Arab colleagues believed that backwardness and corruption would be banished through elections and parliaments, then their successors after 1945 believed that these objects could be attained only if they themselves had power in their hands. With their devotion to the public good and their purity of motive, they would be able totally to remodel society, do away with foreign and native exploitation, give dignity and self-respect to the citizen, banish poverty and set society on the path to increasing prosperity.

From the 1930s onwards, the influence of these European ideologies was manifest in Arab political discourse. The dominant theme in this discourse concerned the necessity, indeed inevitability, of Arab unity. The Arabs, so the argument went, constituted one nation, and should thus be united in one state. Only such a state would preserve the values of Arabism which make an Arab what he is. As the Syrian-born educator, Sati' al-Husri, whom King Faisal put in charge of education in Iraq, put it:

> He who refuses to annihilate himself in the nation to which he belongs may, in some cases, find himself annihilated within an alien nation which may one day conquer his fatherland. This is why I say continuously and without hesitation: Patriotism and nationalism before and above all. . . even above and before freedom.

Sati' al-Husri began formulating his doctrine and spreading it among schoolchildren, university students, and officer cadets before the Second World War. Following the war, his ideas became even more widespread throughout the whole Arab world. A younger generation formulated a variant of Husri's teaching which was even more radical. This variant was the brainchild of a Syrian schoolteacher, Michel Aflaq, who attracted a small group of followers, mostly high-school boys, which he called the Ba'th, i.e., the Resurrection or Renaissance, Party. The group seems to have adopted this name in 1940-41. Aflaq sought a radical refashioning of Arab society. He was like Plato's philosopher-king who had to have an absolutely empty canvas on which to paint the lineaments of a perfect or heavenly society. Aflaq preached a doctrine of love, love for every fellow Arab whose life had to be transfigured. This love, however, required great hatred, hatred and annihilation of everyone who stood in the way of this transfiguration, whether he was an Arab or not.

Some ten years later, the Ba'th Party, which remained very small, was endowed by its leaders with a constitution, the terms of which illustrate clearly the contradiction between constitutional politics and the ideological politics which became increasingly popular in the Arab world from the 1930s onwards. The Ba'th constitution declared its attachment to freedom of speech and assembly, of belief and of artistic creation. The constitution also declared that the people is the source of all authority, and that the unified Arab state for which the Ba'th was working had to be endowed with constitutional and parliamentary government, and had to ensure the freedom of the judiciary.

However, the constitution also declared that the Ba'th was a revolutionary party whose aims could be achieved only through revolution and struggle. The constitution rejected partial and superficial reforms which relied on a slow process of evolution. The party, therefore, was in favor of a three-fold struggle against colonialism and for liberation of the Arab homeland, for unifying the Arabs in a single state, and for the "overthrow of the present faulty structure, an overthrow which will include all the sectors of intellectual, economic, social and political life."

It is obvious that parliamentary government, judicial independence and freedom of speech and assembly are not compatible with a revolutionary struggle designed to turn Arab society, all its institutions, customs, and modes of thought, upside down. In the event, this revolutionary program has failed to be realized in any of its aspects. Ba'thism has conduced not to Arab unification but rather to an increase of tension between the various Arab states, and to a bitter enmity between the two Ba'thist regimes of Iraq and Syria. Neither has Arab society been transfigured or its "faulty structures" replaced or even mended.

In both Syria and Iraq, small Ba'thist parties were enabled to exercise power through military *coups d'état* carried out by officers who were Ba'thist, as in Syria, or persuaded to act in partnership with the Ba'th, as in Iraq. The pursuit of Ba'thist revolutionary aims has meant the establishment of one-party regimes in which rulers use the party network as an adjunct to intelligence and security services in order to control the population in all aspects of its activities and to mobilize it in support of the regime.

The phenomenon of one-party regimes, a contradiction in terms, may be seen not only in Syria and Iraq, but elsewhere in the Arab world. Shortly after the military *coup d'état* which ended the monarchy and abolished political parties in Egypt, the military regime set up a succession of political organizations fully under its control and which were given a monopoly of political action. The Arab Socialist Union was the last of these so-called parties under Nasser. His successor, Sadat, abolished the Union and licensed a number of parties to replace it. Of these, the only one of any consequence is the National Democratic Party, which is the government party and which has allocated to it the lion's share of places in the national assembly.

Libya and the Sudan emulated Nasser in setting up their own Arab Socialist Unions, following military *coups d'état*. One-party regimes were also founded elsewhere in the Arab world. In Algeria, the *Front de Libération Nationale*, which had carried on the armed struggle against the French from 1954 to 1962, and to whom de Gaulle delivered Algeria when he decided to liquidate the French position, established a monopoly of rule which generally went unchallenged until 1988.

In Tunisia, where the French protectorate came to an end in 1954, the leader of the anti-French struggle, Habib Bourguiba, took over and remained the sole ruler until he was deposed by a military *coup d'état* in 1987. The party of which he was the leader, ironically called the Neo-

Destour, i.e., the Neo-Constitutionalist Party, became the only legal party in Tunisia.

In all these regimes, it is not only party organization which is monopolized. State monopoly extends to the media, whether printed or electronic, to publishing, and generally to education, where teachers are employees of the state and curricula and textbooks are also minutely prescribed by the state. This being the case, it is difficult to imagine the circumstances in which democracy can emerge.

To use a term which has been applied to Soviet-style regimes, the rulers of these one-party states constitute a *nomenklatura* in which all decisions are concentrated, and which disposes, at its discretion, of the resources of the state. These resources, in oil-producing states, are very large indeed, and the *nomenklatura's* power thus also becomes correspondingly large. Arab critics have also used another very expressive term to describe these regimes. They have called their rulers Mamelukes, alluding to the slave-soldiers who exercised unrestrained and arbitrary power in those countries, notably Egypt, where they had come to be employed.

The official ideology of the regimes, as has been stated, is pan-Arabism, or the belief that Arabs, constituting a single nation, have to be united in one state. As has been seen, the actual state of affairs in the Arab world has militated against the realization of Arab unity. The various interests are too disparate and too conflicting for unity to come about. The experience of the short-lived United Arab Republic, between 1958 and 1961, is a case in point. It was brought about by Syrian Army officers who were in control of Syria in order to realize the dreams of Arab unity and to seek protection for themselves against domestic and perhaps also external threats. Nasser agreed to the proposed union and assumed that he would be the absolute master in Syria as he had become in Egypt. He sent one of his fellow conspirators in the *coup d'état* of 1952, a major who had become a field marshal, to be his viceroy in

Damascus. The field marshal failed to detect a conspiracy by disgruntled Syrian officers, who had never expected to be sidelined in their own country, and he and his fellow Egyptians had to leave in ignominy.

One of the lessons of this brief episode was that Arab solidarity had very shallow roots and evoked no great loyalty, for all the constant indoctrination by figures like Husri, Aflaq and their followers. The notion that the fundamental loyalty of the Arabs should go to Arabism was novel. People were, of course, aware that they spoke Arabic, but the immense majority of Arabic speakers, who were Muslims, believed that the most important thing about themselves was precisely that they were Muslims. There was, of course, no necessary contradiction between Arabism and Islam. The contradiction appeared where the ideology of Arabism sought to supersede Islamic loyalties and where regimes which sought legitimacy by promoting this ideology were seen to fail in delivering the shining future which the ideology promised, or even a modicum of prosperity and welfare. It is then that the Islamic option became viable and indeed attractive.

This option is not something new in the Arab world. It dates at least from half a century ago when Hassan al-Banna founded in Egypt the Society of the Muslim Brothers. Banna's original purpose was benevolent and philanthropic. He saw masses of Egyptian migrants from the countryside coming to the cities in search of a livelihood. The conditions in which they then found themselves were miserable, both materially and spiritually. Opportunities for employment in cities may have been better, but the migrant fellah was uprooted from his village environment and exposed to penury in urban slums much worse than the worst rural conditions. Even worse, poor men in the city became disoriented, unaware of what they were, and deprived of the welfare which it was the duty of mosques and men of religion to provide. They were, in short, becoming pulverized into a social dust.

Banna saw it as his duty to remedy this state of affairs and set about organizing institutions of self-help and religious guidance for these deprived and forgotten members of society. This deplorable and distressing state of affairs, the Supreme Guide of the Muslim Brothers (as he came to be known) ascribed to the neglect by society and its leaders of the tenets of Islam and of the rules which ought to preside over a healthy Islamic society.

This happened because the greed and corruption spread by European godless unbelievers had come deeply to permeate and poison the very springs of Muslim society. Only a return to the fundamentals of Islam, Banna held, could save and revive the moribund Muslim society. The fundamentals of Islam were not hidden or mysterious. They were to be found in the Koran and the Traditions of the Prophet. As the slogan of the Brethren has it: Islam is our banner and the Koran our constitution.

Unlike the political parties set up by the westernized political class, whether it was the Wafd or the Liberal Constitutionalist or other ephemeral groupings, the Society of the Muslim Brothers was a grassroots organization, evoking devotion and enthusiasm in the mass of the population in whom Banna's preaching found an echo and an answering chord. Nobody knows exactly the size of the Society's membership which, in the decade following its foundation in 1929, grew by leaps and bounds, but it must have numbered hundreds of thousands.

If Islam was to be the banner and the Koran the constitution of Muslim society, certain conclusions had to follow. The Prophet had been not only a prophet, but also a ruler and a war leader. Thus, it was only by the state itself becoming Islamic through and through that Islamic society would find salvation. Necessarily, therefore, the Society became a primarily political organization, dedicated to the pursuit of political power, because only through control of the state institutions would society return to the wholesome Islamic mores of the Prophet's day. Banna, sitting at the apex of this very large organization, decided to use it for realizing the Islamic program. During the war, with the British firmly in control of security in Egypt, the scope for political action was limited. The situation was otherwise after 1945.

In the aftermath of the war, social and political tension was relentlessly on the rise in Egypt, and Banna began to take an active part in the political maneuverings and struggles. It was not only that he was able to mobilize his large following for overt action in the streets, but he had also set up a secret armed apparatus which he used to terrorize and occasionally assassinate prominent political figures. In 1949, a Muslim Brother assassinated the Prime Minister. Shortly afterwards, in retaliation, Banna himself was assassinated. Banna's aspiration to establish a pure Islamic society, and the violence which he came in the end to favor in order to realize his vision, are a striking example of the style of ideological politics so familiar in European history following the French Revolution, a style summed up in Robespierre's belief that virtue without terror is impotent.

This is, therefore, to say that like the other ideologies current in the Arab world, pan-Arabism or Ba'thism, Islamic fundamentalism, as it has come to be generally called, has to be hostile to constitutional and representative government. It will be recalled that the same majority polled by *al-Ahram* which declared in favor of democracy also declared in favor of a *Sharia*-governed society, even though those who were polled did not see that the desire for democracy and the desire for rule by the *Sharia* are utterly incompatible and irreconcilable. In modern society, constitutional and representative government is predicated on a society in which differences of outlook and belief are taken for granted, along with the potential disagreements and conflicts which it is precisely the function of representative government to mediate and reconcile. Hence, the irresistible logic of representative government entails the secularity of the state. Fundamentalism can have no truck with the variety of beliefs and opinions which characterize modern society. Muslim society, however, not being isolated from modern currents of thoughts, will, sooner or later, to some extent or another, exhibit the same variety of belief and opinion. Fundamentalism desires, on the contrary, uniformity of belief and works to enforce the truth at whatever cost to oneself and to others which may prove necessary.

The record of the Muslim Brothers in Egypt following Banna's assassination shows that this essentially popular protest movement directed against misgovernment and oppression by the rulers sought total power for itself as the only efficacious remedy for social and political ills. After the military *coup d'état* of 1952, the Brothers were in hopes that the new regime, which included officers who had sympathized with, or even belonged to, the movement, would move to institute the godly rule for which it hankered. The Brothers were sorely disappointed. The new rulers, led by Nasser, were willing neither to accept the Brothers' ideology nor to allow them even a share of power.

In October 1954, a member tried to assassinate Nasser while he was giving a public speech. The attempt failed and a terrible persecution fell on the Brethren. Their leaders were arrested, tried and given very heavy sentences. The Society was proscribed, and suspected members and sympathizers pursued and interned in large numbers in concentration camps. One of those imprisoned was Sayyid Qutb, who was to be the most important intellectual figure produced by the movement. He was a talented and voluminous writer who very successfully theorized the movement's views and preferences and provided a reasoned and most persuasive case for its program. He remained in prison until 1965. He was briefly released, then rearrested, tried, condemned to death and executed in 1966.

The reason for this harsh treatment was that he published a small book, part of a much larger work of Koranic exegesis, in which he argued that existing Islamic states, so-called, were really living in the Age of Ignorance, the idolatry from which the Prophet was sent to deliver the world. Today's rulers of Islamic countries are aping the idolatry manifest in both the Western and the Communist world, the essence of which is to deny the sovereignty of God and to confer sovereignty on merely human institutions.

This idolatry has infected everything: culture, art, literature, personal relations. It is the rulers who are most responsible for the spread of idolatry, and to extirpate it requires nothing less than the extirpation of these so-called Muslims, who were in reality apostate rulers, and their replacement by a true Islamic order. It is no wonder that Nasser's regime found such arguments to be dangerously subversive and their author to deserve execution.

Qutb's, then, was an activist and radical theory which constituted an overt incitement to the destruction of existing regimes. The manner of his death gave his ideas the halo of martyrdom and attracted groups of followers, who formed extremist off-shoots of the Muslim Brethren, who organized in secret and worked to overthrow the existing regime which they looked upon as an apostate regime, oppressive and an offense to God's majesty. Of these small groups, the one which became best known was that which organized the assassination of President Anwar al-Sadat at the hands of an Army officer. Having done the deed, the officer exclaimed that he had killed the Pharaoh. This was a reference to Pharaoh as he figures in the Koran where he is the embodiment of tyranny and unbelief.

The group to which this officer belonged took its inspiration from a mentor whose ideas were contained in a short pamphlet, *The Forgotten Obligation*. The obligation which Muslims have now forgotten, according to this work, is that of levying war on and killing the Muslim ruler who collaborates with unbelievers to the detriment of Islam. Sadat was such a ruler, *ergo* he was deserving of death. Sadat's assassination was the signal for an uprising by sympathizers, particularly in Upper Egypt, but the authorities succeeded in quickly suppressing it.

Fundamentalism also offered a formidable challenge to the Ba'thist regime in Syria, where the Muslim Brothers had also established themselves. Here their opposition to the regime was even more dangerous than in Egypt. Since the 1960s, Syria has been ruled by Alawite military officers. The Alawites constitute a small minority in an overwhelmingly Sunni population which considered the Alawites as heretics beyond the pale and looked down upon them as a poor peasantry which had never exercised power or shared in government, which was a Sunni appanage. When the servants now became the masters, and when the masters ruled brutally and corruptly, Sunnis, in protest, inclined to lend an ear to the preaching of the Brethren who denounced the secularist Ba'th as the enemy of Islam. The Muslim Brothers posed a formidable challenge to the Ba'thist regime and were in consequence persecuted ruthlessly and suppressed bloodily.

The climax of the long duel between the regime and the Muslim Brothers was the Hama uprising of February 1982, when the regime sent in its troops, airplanes and tanks, decimated the rebels and the population among whom they were ensconced to the tune, it is said, of 20,000 dead, and razed to the ground large parts of the city. It is safe to say that had the Muslim Brothers won, they would have wreaked as great a destruction on the Ba'th and their followers. Here were two absolutist ideologies in confrontation, and between them no space was left at all for constitutional government even to breathe.

The same state of affairs obtains elsewhere in the Arab world wherever established regimes disappoint expectations and allow scope to fundamentalist movements to preach a salvationist gospel to a population predisposed to sympathy owing to its deep Muslim loyalties, and its familiarity with the Islamic discourse adopted by these movements.

This is the case both in Tunisia and Algeria. In Tunisia, Bourguiba ruled supreme between 1954 and 1987, when he was toppled by a military *coup d'état*. Bourguiba strongly favored secularism, in the belief that only by breaking the shackles of traditional Islam would Tunisia become a self-sustaining and prosperous society. Though his was a one-party state, his regime could not compare in ferocity with that of the Ba'th in Syria or Iraq. Yet, secularism had shallow roots and did not satisfy. Fundamentalism was a reaction by new generations to a regime which had become hidebound and in which increasing numbers of the educated class simply no longer felt at home. During the 1980s, Bourguiba and his successor have been challenged and their regime attacked by small groups who proclaimed the same ideal as the Egyptian Muslim Brothers, and the rulers have reacted by imprisoning and suppressing these opponents. Here too, then, there seems no possible room for compromise between the opposing sides.

In Algeria, the clash between the state and the fundamentalists is much more bitter and explosive. The *Front de Libération Nationale* (FLN) has ruled Algeria since 1962, and the results of their rule have not been particularly brilliant. Even though it benefited from oil royalties which were considerably enhanced after 1973, the regime failed to provide employment for the steadily increasing population, and it has failed to enhance welfare and prosperity, the low level of which the FLN had claimed to be the consequence of French colonialism. When it took over from the French, the FLN instituted a command economy which would bring about socialism. The result was a vexatious bureaucracy in the coils of which initiative and innovation were strangled. The hand of this bureaucracy, which constituted a privileged *nomenklatura*, was heavy, enforcing a stifling doctrinal orthodoxy, which the failure of the regime served, however, to discredit. As in Egypt and elsewhere, fundamentalism was a protest couched in familiar Islamic terms against prevailing conditions. These conditions led in 1988 to serious riots which considerably jolted the regime. The following year, in provincial and local elections, the Islamic Salvation Front, which had been active during the 1980s and had, in consequence, suffered repression, obtained majorities in a number of municipalities and provincial councils. The fact that they could do so indicated that the regime was willing to allow the population to give vent to their feelings in the hope this relaxation in turn would dampen discontent. The Islamic Salvation Front and its sympathizers looked upon these results as a triumph, inciting them to push harder in the hope of toppling the regime.

Announcement of general elections in 1991 led to riots, serious disorders requiring Army intervention, and widespread curfews in Algiers and elsewhere. These national legislative elections were finally held in December 1991. In the first round, candidates of the Islamic Salvation Front were returned in an overwhelming majority, while the FLN was miserably routed. Before the second round could take place, the army took over, cancelled the second round, started to arrest the Salvation Front leaders and to suppress any manifestations of support for them and of opposition to the regime. In Algeria, then, as in Egypt, Syria and Tunisia, it is not a question of a government and an (Islamic) opposition working within a mutually acceptable framework of parliamentary institutions; rather it is that the two parties are locked in a gladiatorial combat in which the weaker party must face destruction.

Another issue brings out the incompatibility of fundamentalism and constitutional politics. The issue concerns the place of non-Muslims in an Islamic polity. Traditionally, non-Muslims have occupied an inferior position in a Muslim state. Western-style constitutions have, however, made provision for the political equality of all citizens, regardless of religion. These, however, have remained pro-forma statements, with little or no practical significance. What is significant is that Westernization has also meant the introduction of legal codes which do not discriminate between Muslims and non-Muslims in the administration of the law and which have replaced the punishments prescribed in the *Sharia*, such as mutilation and stoning, for criminal offenses. The rise and spread of fundamentalism has exacerbated inter-communal hostility, and has led to widespread fears that a fundamentalist regime would worsen the status and position of non-Muslims and make them subject to Muslim law.

Egypt has a very large Coptic community. According to official estimates, they form about ten percent of the population, while the Copts themselves claim that they are double this figure. This means that in a population of over 50 million, their numbers would vary from about 6 million to about 12 million. In the tense period preceding President Sadat's assassination in 1981, when fundamentalist antagonism to the regime was particularly acute, fundamentalist hostility to the Copts led to attacks on churches, to anti-Coptic incitements and intercommunal clashes, particularly in Cairo and in Upper Egypt where Copts are especially numerous. Nor has the antagonism abated during the following decade. The reason is not far to seek. Fundamentalists are in earnest about making the *Sharia* the law of the land, and therefore opposed to the alleviation of the unbeliever's inferior status which the replacement of the *Sharia* by European-style legal codes has effected.

The Sudan is another case in point. Like Iraq and Syria, the Sudan is also a heterogeneous country in which one element rules over other elements which are unwilling to accept its dominance. About a third of the Sudanese population, concentrated in the south, is Christian or pagan. It finds itself in a polity dominated by the Muslim

North, because the Republic is the heir of the Anglo-Egyptian Sudan, a territory which Mohammed Ali had conquered and annexed to Egypt. From the start, the place of the South in the Republic has been problematic and troublesome. The South was, from the beginning of independence, afraid of Northern Muslim domination, a fear such that it led to a civil war which raged for 17 years until Colonel Numayri, who had come to power by a military *coup d'état* in 1969, effected a reconciliation with southern leaders in 1972.

However, in the late 1970s, Numayri, fearing for his position, thought to attract support for his regime by co-opting the Muslim Brothers into his government. In 1983, he went further and proclaimed that the *Sharia* was to be the law of the land and to apply to the whole of the land. This was one very potent reason why the civil war reignited in the south. Numayri fell in 1985. A transitional military council took over, which was followed by a civilian government, which was itself toppled by a military *coup d'état*. None of the governments which followed Numayri was prepared to rescind his edict regarding the supremacy of the *Sharia*, and the current military regime is as determined to apply it as Numayri himself. The civil war goes on. In the Sudan, it is not so much that a fundamentalist regime has gained power, as that a military regime has embraced, for its own reasons, fundamentalist positions. In such a situation, a constitutionalist polity becomes doubly out of the question.

Conclusion

This survey of what might be called the varieties of democratic experience in the Arab world cannot but give a dismal impression. This is because the successive attempts to institute constitutional and parliamentary government were generally made in good faith. Their realization was believed to be practicable and to lead, moreover, to the prosperity and happiness of the countries which adopted them. Regardless, however, of aspirations and good intentions, the failure was uniform—a failure reminding one of the Latin poet's rueful confession that he saw and approved what was best, yet ended up following the worst.

To what may this fatality be ascribed? First and foremost, no doubt, to the fact that these ideas of constitutionalism and representation belonged to, and had their rise in, a political tradition and in political arrangements very different from those to which these countries had been long accustomed. What they had been accustomed to was autocracy and passive obedience. This political tradition was, of course, not much different from that of the Sassanids or the Byzantines whom the Islamic empire superseded. These are manners of attending to politics which have a long history and which extend far beyond the realms of the Sassanids, the Byzantines or the Muslims. The poet Valéry described Europe as a peninsula of Asia. It is in this relatively small peninsula that a very different political tradition developed which, because of the great power and prestige of the West in modern times, attracted imitation and emulation which the record now shows to have been ill-judged, and perhaps in most cases even nefarious.

Yet another reason for the failure of the Western constitutionalist tradition to take in the Middle East was that a newer Western political tradition, that of enlightened absolutism, had become familiar to the modernizing Middle Eastern rulers of the nineteenth century. This other Western tradition, with its *penchant* for centralized control, chimed in much more easily with, indeed powerfully reinforced, the native autocratic tradition.

Such are the general causes of the failure. Each country, however, has its own particular tale of failure to relate. In Egypt, it is Zaghlulist populism vying with the rival and incompatible ambition of the royal court which doomed parliamentary government. In Iraq, it is the extreme heterogeneity of the state, which was devoid of any common loyalty binding the population, which put out of question parliamentary government. To this has to be added the pan-Arab ambitions of the regime which the Shi'i and Kurdish majority considered alien and dangerous. All this meant that the regime had to follow violent courses entirely at variance with constitutional government. In Syria the attempt at constitutional and representative government, free of foreign tutelage, lasted much less than in Egypt and Iraq, from 1943 to 1949, when it was overwhelmed by successive military interventions which the political notables who had taken over from the French mandatory government were quite powerless to prevent. In Lebanon, the constitution attempted a balance between various groups, and the army was never a threat to constitutional government. Here, however, the promise of parliamentary rule was finally blighted and destroyed by the weakness of Lebanon vis-à-vis its neighbors, whose designs and ambitions it was unable to withstand, and by the ambitions of its political leaders, which they sought to satisfy by the misuse of elections and the corrupt use of patronage.

The breakdown of a constitutional order, or rather its violent destruction in all the countries mentioned above, as well as in Sudan and Libya, where comparable vicissitudes afflicted the polity, has been followed by ideological politics, whether secularist or fundamentalist, which provide no alleviation for the ills of the Arab world, nor can promise anything but heavy-handed rule conducive neither to welfare, nor to freedom, nor to prosperity. On the other hand, those who say that democracy is the only remedy for the Arab world disregard a long experience which clearly shows that democracy has been tried in many countries and uniformly failed. Until European ideas and the European example spread in the Middle East, the Arab world together with the rest of the Middle East was governed by regimes which were no doubt despotic, but whose methods were understood and accepted. Those methods were discredited and irremediably damaged by the power and influence of Europe. Nothing as lasting, or even as satisfactory, has succeeded in replacing them.